Safi Nidiaye

The Keys to the Heart Method
Shortcut to happiness

Original text in English and German
English Editing and Translation from German:
Peggy Bollmann
Cover Design: Francis Gabriel

Table of Contents

When I open my heart,
I consciously perceive
My own emotions and those of others.
When my heart is closed,
I become their victim.

Introduction

Why are we so often caught up in our unhappiness, our failures, and our guilt, not able to make the right decision or any decision at all? Why do our problems tend to stay as they are and why do so many of our wishes not get fulfilled? Why is it so difficult to change, to become a happier person, to reach one's goals? Is it natural that it's so difficult? Shouldn't it be easier? Shouldn't life be simple?

Many methods and strategies have been developed to help us become happier, healthier, more successful or more able to communicate peacefully with each other. Some of them are based on scientific research. I studied and tried many of them; but whether they were based on neurology, psychology or on spiritual techniques, something was always missing for me. It was either too complicated or not effective enough; there was too much self-violation, or it worked for a while, but did not last long term.

In the end I did find what was missing. It's something extremely simple, yet it makes *all the difference*. When you omit it, nothing you try on the psychological or spiritual path will bring you real change. This simple thing is conscious perception or awareness. Before you can *change* something, you have to *perceive* it. Moreover, it's the perception itself that brings forth the change.

Focused and conscious perception led me onto the path of freedom. Following the path of conscious perception and directed by my intuition, I discovered a method that can resolve almost every life problem, heal our deepest emotional wounds, open our hearts and free us from all the burdens we carry around. And all this without self-violation, without any strategies, without doing anything – besides perceiving. I called this method "Keys to the Heart", or in short "KH" to coincide with the original German name "Körperzentrierte Herzensarbeit". Literally this translates to "body-centred heart work" but could be paraphrased as "getting to the heart of problems via focused body awareness". I wrote several books about this topic, but to date none of them have been translated into English. So, I decided to produce this booklet in English myself in order to make this wonderful path available to English speakers around the world.

May it help you to become what you want to become, to free yourself from the patterns, restrictions and automatisms you are caught in, to resolve your problems, to heal yourself and to unfold your being in freedom and beauty.

The key to everything lies in the heart

If you want to become a better, happier, more successful person, you need to know something about the real nature of emotions. Because it is all a matter of emotions. The key to all your problems is to be found in your heart. You can long and wish for success, happiness or health as much as you want: But if you do not *feel* like someone who is successful, happy or healthy, you probably won't get what you want – or lose it again. According to the law of attraction the way you feel has to be in accordance with what you want to experience. But can you force yourself to feel different from how you really feel? No. You can't. You can try to, but you would suppress your real feelings and the result is that they continue to dominate your attitude.

What does help, however, is to become aware of the feelings you actually have and to take care of them in an adequate way. To consciously perceive a feeling with your heart automatically leads to a change in your inner situation, and every inner change leads to an outer change.

It is emotions that lie behind our striving for success, love, money, fame, or power; it is emotions – often disguised as reason - that make us avoid certain persons or situations or that prevent us from doing what we would like to do; and it is emotions that lead us into conflicts or make us start a war. So, if you want to change your life or your way of reacting, if you want to improve your relationships, resolve your problems and live in peace, you have to switch on the light of your heart, direct it towards your emotions and take care of them. By doing this, you'll discover that there is an infinite number of possibilities for you – instead of the small number of possibilities you think you have.

There are thirteen things that are essential to know about emotions:

1. All our actions and reactions are triggered by emotions, and especially by the deeper, subconscious feelings that we are not aware of.
2. Almost all our problems – individual as well as collective – are caused by the fact that instead of feeling our emotions consciously, we allow them to dominate us subconsciously.
3. We allow our emotions to dominate us because we mistake them for facts, for something that constitutes part of ourselves.
4. But there is no such *thing* as an emotion. What we call "emotion" is just the way we feel about a certain thing in a certain moment.

5. Because an emotion is not an object or a fact, but just a way of feeling, its nature is transient or fleeting. It changes by and of itself. Look at a child: Its state of mind constantly changes – one moment it is full of joy, the next moment it feels sad or annoyed or angry and then again full of hope or joy. So, an emotion is never a problem, unless you mistake it for a fact, something solid that forms part of your being.

6. Because an emotion is not a fact and not something static that stays in our reality forever, but just a way of feeling that changes from one moment to the next, it is of no use to try to overcome it; you just need to feel it and it will automatically make you feel different. By trying to *overcome* an emotion, it becomes something solid, like water that turns into ice. Neither is it necessary to *heal* emotions as there is nothing sick about them; they are just ways of feeling in a certain moment about a certain thing and they always have their reason and their purpose. Nor do you have to *accept* your emotions if you don't want to. All you need to do is to feel them. That's what makes your soul alive: actually, em*body*ing your feelings.

7. Once you discover an emotion and start feeling it consciously, it will no longer dominate you.

8. An emotion (or way of feeling) that is not felt consciously stays in your body. In other words, the body is the place where your un-felt emotions get stored and can always be found again by attentively tuning in to your body.

9. By feeling an emotion in your body, you start opening your heart to this emotion.

10. By opening your heart to an emotion, you give it the right place and the care it needs. Then, instead of dominating you and making you unhappy, this emotion will reveal its purpose to you.

11. Many of the emotions you are suffering from are not your own; they belong to someone else – parents, partners, people you meet. Unconsciously we often take on other people's feelings. If you are stuck in a problem or a pattern, the reason might be that you are acting out a drama that is not yours.

12. You can free yourself from those foreign emotions by realising that they don't belong to you. This is like "giving them back" to the person they belong to.

13. The key to almost every problem in your life lies within your heart.

Chapter One

The Power of Conscious Perception

I didn't like my reality.
I tried to change it.
The more I tried
The more it resisted.
Then I gave up struggling against it
and started watching.
Just watching.
Then it began to change.

How to deal with difficult situations

Something happens. It makes you unhappy. Or angry. You don't want to be unhappy or angry. So, you try to change the situation. Or the other person. Or your emotion. Or yourself.

But the situation is difficult to change; and even if you happen to be able to change it, you will soon encounter the same kind of situation again. That's because it's not the situation that is the problem; the problem lies within yourself.

Neither can you make the other person change; maybe she agrees to change her behaviour for a while, and you think your problem is resolved. But tomorrow she will fall back into her old behaviour, and if not, another person with a similar pattern will pop up in your life and you become angry or unhappy again. It's because the other person is not the cause of your anger or unhappiness; the cause is inside you.

Maybe you work hard in order to change your own person, your thinking, your feeling or your way of reacting. Maybe it works for a while. But inevitably, one day something will happen that makes you fall back into your old habits and you become angry or unhappy again. This is because the reason of your unhappiness or anger does not lie in who you are, or in how you feel or how you act. The real reason lies somewhere else: a lack of awareness.

It all starts with awareness. Without awareness nothing works. Not on the spiritual path, not in the realm of psychological healing. Without awareness you will not be able to resolve your real problems, attain your real goals or find fulfilment.

What do I mean by "real problems"? You might happen to change the situation that you don't like, but the real problem is generally not the outer situation but your inner landscape. The way you think and feel. Unless you awaken from it, your life problem will not go away – or you will encounter the same kind of situation again and again.

What do I mean by "real goals"? Your real goal is that which lies *behind* your striving, your wishes and desires. The nostalgia that manifests itself through your wishes. For example, you desperately want to have this specific work, thing or person; yet if you look deeper, you will find that it is not the object, person or work that this is all about, but the way you would *feel* by getting what you want. So, you might happen to get a wish fulfilled, a goal achieved, but the nostalgia stays unless you attain your "real goal" – which is a feeling.

What is more - this feeling is of no use for you if you don't feel it consciously. Only conscious awareness will help you to attain your real goal. On the spiritual path, if you don't have awareness or the capacity of conscious perception, you might experience very nice moments, you will from time to time be uplifted, get intuitions or inspirations, maybe believe that you are enlightened – but in reality, you move into a sphere of fantasies. Real illumination is based upon sober, conscious perception.

So, this is our starting point: First of all, you have to discover what it means to perceive something consciously, objectively, without interpreting it or being identified with any idea about it.

Awaken conscious perception or awareness and discover the world in a new way

Conscious perception is the most powerful instrument you own. It enables you to discover those thoughts and emotions that are at the root of your problems; it enables you to awaken from them, as one awakes from a bad dream. You might for instance discover that from your earliest childhood you have always been unconsciously convinced that you are worthless. Any situation that reminds you about this "fact" will lead to an emotional reaction; you get angry or sad or you just withdraw. By applying conscious perception, you will discover that "being worthless" is not a fact, but an idea, and by consciously feeling the pain that this idea has caused in you for so many years, your heart will open to this pain. This old emotional wound can start to heal now.

If a similar situation arises again, you will not get angry or sad or get the urge to flee the situation; you will just realise that this is the kind of situation that made you feel hurt before, and no longer react. You will even be able to feel what the other person feels and understand her.

Consciousness is light

Consciousness is light. That of which you are not conscious lies in darkness; that of which you are conscious is visible to you. Most of the thoughts and feelings we have lie in the dark. And that's the reason why they dominate us and make us react in certain ways. Because we are not conscious of our thoughts and feelings, we easily justify our actions to ourselves with reasonable arguments. For instance, I might say to myself that flying to Hawaii is not reasonable because it's too expensive; while in reality I am just afraid of the long flight. But this fear lies in the dark. I am not aware of it. If someone asks me what I'm afraid of, I might answer: *"Me? Afraid? I'm just trying to be reasonable!"*

Or I accept an invitation only because I don't want to hurt the person by refusing; when in reality I don't want to feel guilty or I don't want to be seen as a bad person. My feeling of being guilty or bad lies in the shadow of my consciousness; I am not aware of it. But it is *because* I am not aware of it that it can dominate me. I act like someone who thinks she is bad or guilty and wants to avoid being reminded of that fact. Once I direct the beam of consciousness (=light) towards that feeling of being guilty or bad, I can awake from it – by discovering that it's just a way of feeling and thinking and not a reality. It then can't dominate me anymore.

Shit happens.

(…as we all know, at least since Forrest Gump…)

With the light switched off: You interpret things as you have always interpreted them, according to the way your mind is programmed (mostly in childhood). Your reaction is hardly related to the actual situation, but to a situation in your past.

With the light switched on: You see things as they are, your reaction is directly related to the actual situation.

For example: You meet your neighbour and he walks past you without returning your greeting. Automatically you think that he doesn't like you for some reason or that he looks down upon you. You get angry and the next time you see him, you don't greet him either.

You don't even realise that *"he obviously doesn't like me"* or *"he is stuck up"* are just thoughts that may or may not be true in reality. You also don't realise that this thought triggers a pain in you, and that this pain has been part of you since childhood. Perhaps you have never felt seen and respected, or have always felt put down and worthless.

If, however, you switch on your conscious perception, you will notice immediately, that *"he doesn't like me"* is merely one of your many thoughts, and that this thought is neither a fact nor necessarily true. You will also notice that this thought brings a painful feeling to the surface, allowing you to consciously perceive this previously unconscious emotion. Once you have practised the techniques that I will teach you, this can happen within seconds. This in turn allows you to realise that the only fact in this situation is that your neighbour did not greet you, and that there are literally countless possible reasons for his behaviour. Because of this, there is no need for you to react, because in fact, it is none of your business.

Shit happens.

Light off: You react in an automatic way and you don't have any influence on yourself or the others, or the situation.

Light on: Instead of reacting on auto-pilot, you become aware of your automatic interpretation of the situation and understand that this is just the way you think (instead of believing that it's reality); you see things as they are and then act the way you really want to act. You have influence on yourself; and impact on the situation and the people. Let's look at this in a more dramatic situation.

Let me illustrate this with the example of a married couple, Leila and Fred. First at all I tell you what happened. Then I show you how things could change if Leila switches on the light of conscious perception – and/or if Fred does so.

Example: Leila and Fred

Leila's husband is obviously avoiding her. He hardly makes eye contact anymore and doesn't spend much time at home. Leila becomes suspicious and starts looking through his things in search of evidence for an affair.

One day she finds a restaurant bill for two people and she becomes livid with anger. When she wants to go to a restaurant, he tells her that it is too expensive, yet here he racked up a sizeable bill at a luxury eatery. Her anger and suspicion go round and round in her head and she is certain that his behaviour is out of order. After collecting more pieces of "evidence" she has had enough, confronts him with the "facts" and threatens divorce.

As it turns out, the real reason why Leila's husband has been avoiding her is because he lost his job. Because he fears his wife's anger, and is only too familiar with being called a failure and a loser throughout his childhood, he is desperately trying to secure a new job without telling her anything about it. The expensive restaurant visit was his attempt to convince an old acquaintance to employ him. Neither Leila nor her husband were consciously aware of the thoughts and feelings that triggered their actions.

Let's look at the same story again - this time with Leila switching on the light of conscious perception in time:

Leila notices that her husband avoids eye contact and doesn't spend much time with her anymore. She realises that this makes her feel insecure (as a sense of insecurity was the feeling that gave rise to her suspiciousness displayed in the first version of this story). She allows herself to feel insecure, knowing that she is dealing with a feeling and not with a fact. This opens her heart, which in turn allows her to ask her husband Fred whether there is anything that is occupying his mind. Because her question comes from the heart and is asked with empathy, interest and respect, Fred feels able to tell his wife what has happened. However, in his story of events, he explains that he only lost his job because for once he had dared to tell his boss the truth to his face. He then happened to run into an old acquaintance, who on hearing about his plight invited him to the restaurant and paid for the meal. The bill ended up in Fred's pocket by accident.

Now the same story again, this time with Fred also switching on his light of conscious awareness.

Fred notices that, to him, losing his job means that he is ashamed of himself in front of his wife, that he knows this feeling from his childhood, and that behind this shame is an old pain of feeling like a loser. While becoming conscious of these emotions, he realises that he is dealing with feelings from childhood and not facts in present time. This puts him in the position – even if feeling slightly insecure – of being able to tell Leila the truth: he has lost his job, has felt ashamed and fearful of being seen as a loser by her and so on and so forth...

By the way: had he applied even more consciousness, he could have noticed even more: that the insecurity he felt during their conversation was in fact Leila's insecurity, which he felt subconsciously and mistook as his own feeling.

In the end Leila's and Fred's hearts are open to one another, everything is out in the open and their love has strengthened. Reassured by this love, Fred now radiates self-assurance and confidence, which in turn inspires several employers from whom he had applied for jobs to make him an offer, out of which Fred can now choose the best one.

Conscious perception is a miracle medicine

Conscious perception or awareness will allow you to see things as they are instead of interpreting them in the light of your unconscious convictions and emotions. It will allow you to become free – free from being dependent on persons or circumstances, free from yourself. It will allow you to heal yourself and to find fulfilment. Moreover, it will open your heart so that you are able to develop understanding, compassion and respect for your own feelings, as well as those of others.

All this is achieved by practising conscious perception or awareness, especially when you direct the beam of your conscious perception onto your emotions, because there lies the key to your problems.

What is conscious perception?

Start a little experiment: switch on your light of consciousness – meaning that you set the intention to perceive *consciously* everything that you experience via your senses. Everything you see, for example, or all the noises you can hear. Decide to listen consciously to everything you can hear nearby and everything you can hear in the distance.

Consciously notice your breath.
Consciously notice everything you can smell, everything you can feel in your body and everything you can feel where your body touches something like your clothes, the surface you are sitting or standing on. Take a moment to consciously notice.

Feel your breathing.
Feel your body.
Notice your senses.

This basically equates to a short form of Zen meditation. This is what switching on conscious perception or conscious awareness is all about. You have now switched-on conscious awareness.

Normally our awareness is absorbed by thoughts, hypnotised by a conversation, or a screen (TV, internet, cell phone, cinema) or something we are involved with. So, the first thing you have to learn is to be aware instead of being hypnotised. You can switch on awareness like you switch on a light. Just remember to be aware.

What is the first thing you become aware of once you awaken your awareness? It's the breath. The rise and fall of your breath is always there, whatever happens and wherever you are, and nothing is closer to you than your breath. So, watch your breath. Right now. Stop reading for a while and do nothing but watch your breath. Inhaling, exhaling. Inhaling, exhaling. Don't influence your breath; just watch it.

Now notice from where you are watching your breathing: Are you sitting in your head like in a tower, looking down towards your nose and belly in order to watch your breath? Or are you watching from inside your body, where you perceive your breath? In case of the latter, you are not only watching your breath but you are feeling it.

Feel your breath. Inhaling, exhaling. Feel each breath. Continue reading while feeling your breath. Do you realise how feeling your breath has directed your attention into your body?

Feel your breath and feel your body. Now you are present in your body instead of being caught by thoughts. But still, you are kind of hypnotised. In order to fully awaken into presence, you have to become aware of your sensory perception. Perceive consciously what you hear, smell, see and taste.

But be careful: Don't search for these perceptions, don't turn it into work. Perception is not something you do, but something that happens. All you have to do is to awaken your awareness to what you perceive.

The cat enters, I perceive it.
The floor crackles, I perceive it.
There is an itch on my left foot, I perceive it.
Angry thought about that itch, I perceive it.

Can you see what I mean?
Whatever happens - inside or outside - you just perceive it. It is extremely simple. But as we are not used to perceiving in this way, it appears to be extremely difficult.

Feel your breath.
Feel your body.
Be aware of what you perceive.

Oops, you find yourself absorbed by thoughts…
Don't worry, that's normal. Just return into the present moment.

Feel your breath.
Feel your body.
Be aware of what you perceive.

No need to *do* anything. Just be aware.

For those of you who are used to always being busy this can be hell. It seems boring.

But don't give up. This is Zen meditation. If you practice this regularly, constantly, it might even lead to illumination.

But for our purpose of body and feeling awareness it is merely our starting point, the first step of the exercise. By practising this, you discover that you are able to just watch. You discover the inner place from where you just watch – in a neutral, objective way, without being identified with what you watch.

Practice just a few minutes a day, and your awareness will be awakened and sharpened. You become more alert, more present, better protected from external feelings and influences, more centred. Able to decide what you do instead of reacting automatically. Also, it will provide you a kind of refuge within yourself.

Now: The same kind of conscious awareness that in this exercise is directed at nothing in particular, can also be directed specifically at something: for instance, at your thoughts. At the state of your body that goes with these thoughts. And at the emotions that hide in this state of body.

Chapter Two

How to perceive an emotion without getting lost in it

It's all about emotions.
As long as I did not understand this,
nothing really changed.
The key to my problems, my conflicts,
to all the questions that tortured me:
I found it in my heart.

Thoughts are perceived by observing – emotions are perceived by feeling

Next, you are going to apply that same ability of conscious perception to your emotions.

Contrary to thoughts, which can be observed from a distance, the only way you can perceive a feeling is by actually feeling it. Observation will merely establish that you are having a feeling, and this is not the same as *consciously perceiving* it.

Thoughts are perceived by taking a step back and observing.
Feelings are perceived by immersing yourself in them and actually feeling them.
Body sensations are perceived by sensing them.
Smells are perceived by smelling them.

How does one perceive an emotion? When you are angry – how do you know that you are angry? You know it because you are thinking angry thoughts. Your attention is directed towards that which causes your anger. In order to *perceive* the anger, you have to change the direction of your attention. Instead of directing it towards the situation or the person that makes you angry, you have to direct it towards yourself. The first thing you'll realise when doing so, is your breath and your body. You'll realise that there is tension in your body. Perhaps in your arms, your chin, your legs. Maybe you are breathing more heavily than usually.

Now you are perceiving the expression of anger in your body. But is this the anger itself? While experiencing this bodily state attentively, turn your attention towards yourself: How do *you* feel in this bodily state? Watch your breath while asking yourself this question. Now you are starting to perceive the anger.

Once you start feeling this emotion consciously, it will touch your heart; your heart will open to the emotion and react to it with understanding, compassion and respect.

Once your heart opened to an emotion, you'll find yourself in a completely different state. Before, you were angry; your attention was caught up with angry thoughts and directed towards the person or circumstance that made you angry. Now, your attention is directed towards the feeling of anger and embraces it with respect and understanding. The moment your heart opens to an emotion is profoundly touching - it gives you a feeling of coming home, a moment of love, something intimate and holy. When you look at the person or situation again, you will be able to feel the anger in your heart - as an emotion - but you will no longer identify with it. Instead of making you mad, it gives you a kind of strength and dignity.

Example: The messy table

Every day I find the same disorder on my table — the part of our big, shared table that is supposed to belong to me and no one else, and every day it takes me quite some time to reset order — MY order — on that part of the table. It's not me, it's my husband who causes this disorder. I've told him many times to respect my order; to not touch my papers; so why can't he do what I ask him to do? I am so angry. I have been angry many times over this, I have expressed my anger many times; it did not change anything. Now I start to look at it.

I close my eyes and think of the situation that makes me so angry. Every day the same mess! And this despite the fact that I have addressed this so many times! Anger. OK. I direct my attention inwards, into my own body and I perceive. What can I notice in my body?

Tension. Incredible tension. In my arms, my jaw, my legs, my belly. My whole body feels tense. Behind all this tension sits indignation. I direct my full attention towards it. Breathe it. Feel it. Open my heart to it.

This indignation requires acknowledgement and understanding. More than that: permission to exist, respect.

And finally, some space. Permission to be. Oh yes – now I can sense a shift. Before I wasn't even present, I was totally lost in angry thoughts! Now I feel present and my anger and indignation is also present. But smaller than me. It's just a feeling that is well taken care of by my heart. I notice that my body has become more relaxed and upright. Now I am in a position to talk to my husband without the desire to hurt him, yet still speaking my truth.

But there is more. Opening your heart to a negative emotion like anger, sadness or fear will make you discover the deeper feeling that was hidden behind this emotion: the pain. For instance, the pain of feeling rejected, or humiliated or a victim of injustice. That's how you *really* feel; your anger just tries to protect you from that pain. Once you have opened your heart to this pain, the whole situation will change. It's like awakening from a nightmare.

Let's explore this some more using the above example.

Now I ask myself what actually made me so angry. How do I really feel about this constant mess? What about it causes me so much hurt? The injustice of it all!!! I find it unfair that over and over again I have to clean up the mess that he has created. And – now the real pain suddenly reveals itself – I find it so unfair that I am not listened to. That he doesn't respect what I say. OK. This is the point to really feel again.

Breathe. Feel the body sensations. How do I really feel? Not listened to...overlooked... ignored... No – not considered... not respected. My eyes well up. This is the pain: feeling disrespected. I focus on this feeling, consciously feel this feeling, allow this feeling, give it space. Then my heart opens up to this feeling. It mainly needs to be felt - consciously felt - and to be recognised as a feeling as opposed to a fact.

In the end I can clearly see that it is not a fact, that my husband doesn't respect me. He does respect me. It's just that at the moment he is so concerned about a problem of his own, that he does not even notice when he rearranges the papers on the table. I realise that his entire attention is directed towards finding a solution for his problem, and this insight not only wakes me up out of my anger and my idea that he doesn't respect me, but it also opens my heart for him and his problem. And suddenly a super-simple idea pops into my head that provides a solution: I offer him the use of the whole table and set up another one for myself. Easy! The idea had just never occurred to me before because I was so preoccupied with my anger.

This is quite different from our normal way of dealing with an emotion. Normally, we just *have* the emotion. *"I have this big sadness."* Or we *are* the emotion. *"I am angry."* Perceiving the emotion means: *"I perceive anger." "I feel sadness."* Can you see the difference?

Conscious perception will change everything in your life

Perceiving changes your position, and this change of position will change everything in your life. You will see things in a different way, act in a different way, think in a different way, people will perceive you in a different way, react in a different way, and life will respond to you in a different way.

Acting out of a feeling of anger, or superiority, or revenge or rejection is in the spiritual world often considered as acting out of the "ego".
But in my opinion, there is no such thing as an ego. What we call ego is just our being identified with a certain group of thoughts and emotions. It is of no use to try and fight the ego, or to overcome it, or to heal it. Because it does not exist. Instead of wasting your time and energy attempting this, your time and energy is, in my opinion, much better spent by perceiving what you are identified with in this very moment.
By perceiving it you awake from it.
That's all.

When you are overflowing with anger, perceive this anger.
Perceive the thought that makes you angry.
Perceive the pain that is caused by this thought.

By doing so, this pain will touch your heart and your heart will open to this pain.

Then you are no longer angry, you are no longer identified with the thought that made you angry, and suddenly you will discover all the ideas and perspectives that you could not see until now, because being exclusively identified with one of them made you blind to all the rest.

In this moment you will be able to realise how things really are, and to perceive what the other persons, those who share the situation with you, really think and feel.

So, if you want to be free, happy and successful, or be a better person, all you have to do is to change the inner position. First of all, awake: Switch the light on. Become aware that something is going on inside. Change the direction of your attention – instead of looking at a situation or a person, you turn your attention towards yourself, towards the way you feel.

Herein lies the key to understanding, overcoming, resolving, changing or healing the situation, the problem or yourself.

Being identified with a certain idea and emotion – as we normally are - you will experience life as an endless fight: fighting to reach your goals, to realise your desires, to keep what you own, fighting against your fears, against your ego, your anger, or against the persons or circumstances that make you angry or unhappy.

By applying conscious perception you'll find yourself in a position where there is no need to fight.

Now, let's return to the basic exercise. Conscious perception. Remember?

Feel your breath.
Feel your body.
Watch your sensory perceptions.
Be present.

Now - how can you apply this to an emotion?
Let's look at anger again.
Something happens.
You get angry.
You switch the light on and realise that there is anger.
You turn the direction of your attention inside.
What does it mean to feel this anger?
Feel your breath.
Feel your body.
Decide to get to know this anger.
Where in your body can you perceive it?
Maybe you feel stomach pain. Or tension in your arms, your back, your jaw.

Direct your attention right to the middle of these symptoms and feel your breath.
This is the way you feel the anger.
And this is the beginning of an awakening.

Chapter Three

How to awake from the drama

The situation was intolerable. Unbearable.
I struggled, I cried, I screamed.
Then I turned my attention inwards,
and I discovered that the cause of my trouble
was not the situation, but my thoughts about it.
Thoughts that hurt me.
Opening my heart to that pain changed everything:
myself, my perspective, my feelings
and finally—even the situation.

Awareness is what you need

Opening your heart and feeling your anger consciously instead of being angry is not yet the solution to your problem; it is just the beginning, because your anger has a reason. This reason lies in the deeper feeling hidden underneath the anger.

Why are you angry?

You are angry because you feel hurt. So how do you really feel about this situation? What hurts you so much that you become angry?

Maybe you feel rejected. Or annihilated. Or like a victim of injustice. Or abandoned, or guilty, bad or ugly. Worthless. Not seen, not respected, not heard... Or despised or seen as a loser...

Wherever there is a negative emotion (like anger, sadness, fear), there is pain. The negative emotion tries to protect you from feeling this pain. "Negative" means "saying no" while "positive" means "saying yes" to something. Every negative emotion is a way of saying *"no, I don't want this"*. The thing you don't want is not the outer situation, but the inner pain it triggers in you. This is often a very old feeling, commonly from your childhood.

Once you open your heart to the pain lying at the base of your problem, your perspective changes.

You feel different, see things in a different way.
You are no longer angry.

You have awoken from the drama. There is no drama anymore; the drama only arose because you weren't prepared to feel this pain. But why? Because you were under the impression that it could be dangerous – perhaps even kill you. This idea appeared to be a fact, it appeared to be something that you were – you might have felt that you were being rejected, abandoned, judged, humiliated, for example. Now that you have finally allowed yourself to feel this pain for the first time, you realise that what you were feeling never was a fact, that you never *were* any of those things, but that you were merely *experiencing* an emotion and that this emotion was probably based on a childhood interpretation of a similar situation. Mummy went away, so I must have been bad. Daddy was angry, so I must have been guilty of something. I don't get cuddled, so I must be unlovable or ugly or naughty. The reality is, however, that you *are* not bad or guilty or unlovable, but that you *feel* that way. Your mum leaving, your dad being angry or nobody cuddling you does not turn you into a different person! "Bad", "guilty" and "unlovable" are *feelings*, not facts.

All this you realise when you have discovered the pain underneath your problem, when you have felt this pain, and when you have correctly identified it as a feeling as opposed to a fact. If you then look at the present situation again – the one that appeared to be so terrible – you will notice that you aren't emotionally affected anymore, or at least to a much lesser extent than before.

How to work your way through a problem

In order to really and fully get through a problem, three things must happen in your inner world:

1. Your body must be freed from the tension of the emotion
2. The emotion must be taken into your heart
3. The reason of the emotion must be dissolved.

The consequences in the outer world? We'll see to that later. First take care of yourself and then return to the outer situation. And don't worry, there *will* be a change in the outer world too.

Let's start with the body.

1. The body must be freed from the tension of the emotion

Our thoughts and emotions find their expression in our body.

We are not accustomed to consciously perceiving our thoughts and emotions. Instead of simply paying attention to them, we usually act them out in words or deeds. What is worse, there are many emotions that we don't even allow ourselves to act out – they are suppressed out of principle and we never become aware of them at all.

Yes – it is possible to push feelings aside, to ignore them, to banish them from our heart by refusing to feel them, respect them and be compassionate towards them. Yet what we can't avoid, is for our feelings to leave their mark on our body, because the way our feelings express themselves via our physical being is not subject to our will.

Feelings influence how our blood circulates through our veins, how fast our heart beats, how well our digestion works, how energies make their way through meridians and how electrical impulses are transmitted via neural pathways. Biologically, the autonomous nervous system – the one that (with the exception of a few highly developed yogis) we cannot control with our free will, governs most of these processes.

This means that if you want to bring those feelings into your consciousness that you are not, or not sufficiently aware of, but that nevertheless have an overwhelming influence on your thoughts and your body, you need to direct your attention inwards. Yet it is not sufficient to just *detect* your body sensations and feelings, you need to *experience* them. This is achieved by feeling your feelings at the same time as observing your breath. In this way you not only notice them superficially, but you touch them, penetrate them with your presence, with your breath and your attention. In this way you coax them out of their hiding places inside your body into the light of consciousness and in the end, you bring them into your own heart – which has always been the place where feelings belong.

2. The emotion must be taken into your heart

When I say "heart", I mean the spiritual core of our being – not the physical organ. This core of our being is where our inner experience takes place, it's the place where we feel, where we are touched by events, beings, emotions or whatever we encounter, and also where we are in touch with our soul, our deeper stirring, our nostalgia, our truth. If your heart is closed, nothing can touch you - you are like a stone, or a machine such as a computer. If your heart is open you feel. Feeling means perceiving fully, through contact. So, we are touched by what we feel. It moves us. It causes" emotion"(= a way of being moved).

This is why we often try to close our heart. We feel threatened. Some emotions appear dangerous to us, as if they threatened us and our very survival, so we close our hearts to them. Other emotions are simply not allowed – it seems to us as if it was not proper to feel them. This is often due to our experiences as children, when we were forbidden to express certain feelings. In reality no feeling can harm, let alone kill us – yet that is not how it seems to us. When we mistake feelings for facts it can appear as if they were truly dangerous.

To reiterate: no feeling can hurt us or threaten our survival – because feelings are "just" feelings. The word "just" in this case is not intended to be a value judgement, but merely to highlight that we are NOT dealing with a fact, but rather a fleeting state of being in reaction to a certain event. As long as you can perceive the event and your related feelings about it consciously, nothing terrible is going to happen.

Suppose you suddenly notice hate arising within you. If you've already had a bit of practice in conscious perception you should be able to "catch" this feeling of hate arising just in time before it submerges again into the darkness of your subconscious. To hate is considered to be a "bad" thing, but to consciously perceive the feeling of hate is not a bad thing at all. You study this hate with great interest; you consciously experience what hate feels like in your physical body and all the while you know that it is "just" a feeling. When you feel this feeling of hate with genuine interest, attention and patience you *will* experience your heart opening up to it. Understanding and compassion for this feeling of hate will naturally arise within you. At the same time, you get in touch with the deeper feeling sitting behind the hate – your pain. A pain so bad, that in order to protect yourself from it, you have had to resort to hate.

Your heart's natural reaction to *any* genuine feeling will always be understanding, respect, compassion, acknowledgement, and empathy - it has no choice, because it can feel it through and through...

The reason for the emotion must be dissolved

Whenever there is a negative emotion there is pain. You are not just angry - you are angry because you feel hurt, for instance because of humiliation or injustice. You are not just sad, you are sad about a pain, for instance the pain of being abandoned or having lost something or someone. You are not just afraid, but you are afraid of something that makes you feel hurt. The real feeling underneath negative emotions is always some kind of pain.

Now - what turns a situation into a problem is not the pain itself, but the fact that you reject it. You don't want it. And the reason you don't want it, is that you don't know that it is a feeling. You mistake it for a fact, for something that you are. For instance, subconsciously you mistake "humiliation" for a fact that concerns you, that turns you into another person, instead of realising that it is the way you feel. You are identified with this feeling. It is this identification that creates your problems.

So, when I say that the reason for the emotion must be dissolved, I don't mean that the situation must be changed – but that you must wake up from the false identification with your pain and with the negative thought which lies behind it. The thought of being worthless, unloved, being a victim of injustice and so forth.

How can you wake up from such a negative conviction? By noticing it and realising that it is a thought, not a reality. When you catch yourself having such a thought, avoid declaring this thought "wrong", but simply recognise it for what it is: a thought.

Yet the intellectual insight *"this is merely a thought"* is unfortunately not quite enough to really snap yourself out of it. Your intellect might concede – theoretically – that the thought *"I am worthless"* is not a fact, but a (childish) idea. However, the *feeling* connected to this thought – the pain of feeling worthless – is anchored deep within your psyche and within your physical body, and it is for the purpose of awakening you from this identification, that you must feel this pain consciously.

Only after feeling this pain will you *actually* know that you are dealing with a thought or emotion and not a fact. This is a huge awakening – comparable to deleting a glitch in the programming of your operating system at the root of your thinking and feeling. You will notice that you now look at everything with new eyes, you might perhaps even have become a new person.

Example: Anita goes nuts

Anita enjoys a deep and loving relationship with her husband, yet whenever he appears withdrawn to her and cool without any apparent reason, she literally goes nuts.

She simply can't bear it and reckons that it is just not right that, completely out of the blue, he would avoid connection, smiles, eye contact and kisses, sport a sour face and reduce his communication to the bare minimum. It throws Anita into a rage. She feels as if she can't reach him at all anymore and she can't stand it.

When she sits down to go inwards and investigate, she first notices a restlessness in her body and underneath it the feeling that she can't bear it. This feeling needs compassion, space and to be recognised as a feeling as opposed to a fact. Now she calms down a little bit. Anita asks herself which feeling it is that she can't bear. To identify this feeling, she re-lives the situation. She is hit by a wave of pain, accompanied by uncontrollable sobbing.

Anita decides not to be overcome by this wave of emotion, but observes it attentively, feels it consciously. Her whole body convulses. She allows herself to experience these convulsions, this sobbing, these waves of pain, and it takes quite a while before she can finally name the feeling that is so powerfully moving through her: it is the feeling of being cut off.

After opening her heart to this feeling, she realises that this is the feeling she felt as a young child, when her mother withdrew into her depression. While her mother managed to take care of Anita's bodily needs, she was otherwise not reachable to her. Anita realises that this feeling of being cut off has nothing to do with her marriage; her husband's behaviour has simply brought this painful, buried feeling from her childhood into her consciousness.

Thus, awoken out of her identification with feeling cut off, Anita can now see her initial situation with new eyes. She now has access to her husband's heart and can sense how he feels. She can see that the reason why he has retreated within himself is that he is absorbed by a problem that he is trying to solve.

In the following weeks Anita notices that she has generally become more awake to the feelings and issues of others. She had never realised to what extent her conviction of being cut off had indeed cut her off from real contact.

Chapter Four

The Practice Part

I sit calmly.
I watch my breath, feel my body.
I watch my thoughts: What are they about?
What's the issue that wants to be looked at
in this moment?
How does my body react to these thoughts?
Which emotion is expressed
by this bodily reaction?
What does this emotion need from me?
I sit calmly and watch.
Feel my breath, feel my body.

Let's make it concrete now

Having covered the theory, let's now tackle practical considerations. This chapter is divided into two parts:

Part 1
The Steps of the "Keys to the Heart" process:

1. Initial overview of the steps (i.e., this is not enough   to get started yet)
2. Commentary on each step, which you should definitely read before getting started
3. Detailed instructions for each step
4. A case study
5. Summary sheets to refer to as a reminder of the steps

Part 2
How to work through a problem situation:

1. The effect of the first step: discovering a feeling
2. How to identify the underlying pain of a feeling
3. Every problem includes a longing
4. Discovering the good feeling contained in any longing

5. The different layers of a problem and how we know that we have gone through all of them
6. The role of breathing

Initial overview of the „Keys to the Heart" process

You want to get to the bottom of a problem situation in order to solve it. Put simply: what turns a situation into a problem is the way you *feel* about it but don't want to. Therefore, in order to solve your problem, you must:

- Become consciously aware of the feelings (or emotions, which in my language is the same) that currently dominate you in this situation. You discover those feelings by noticing what your physical body does in response to them.
- Stop identifying with those feelings and start observing them consciously. This you do by withdrawing your attention from the outer situation and turning it inwards. By tuning into your physical body, you explore and familiarise yourself with your feelings. This will help you realise that your feelings are not facts, not you, and not permanent.
- Feel your emotion, immerse yourself in it. Because a feeling has to be felt to be perceived, you can't just observe it like a thought. Feeling a

feeling takes place in your heart. To enable this, you first need to open the various locks with which - way back when - you have bolted the door to your heart shut, in order to protect yourself from the pain connected to the feeling. These locks open when you find the correct keys – i.e., you need to find whatever it is that your feelings need in order to be perceived completely, but so far haven't received yet.

The ultimate aim is to be able to experience a similar situation without falling back into identifying with the feeling – or in other words, to enter a similar situation as a new person with a new way of looking at the situation and with a new way of reacting to it. To check whether you have achieved this aim, you simply conjure up the situation again vividly in your imagination.

Whenever you discover feelings in you that on closer inspection are not actually yours, you need to re-direct them straight back to where they belong: the person you took them on from.

The technique is simple: you direct your attention

- first to the thoughts and images related to your situation
- then to the reaction of your physical body

- then to the emotion that you discover underneath your physical reaction
- then to the way your emotions react to the keys you are offering to open your heart
- and finally, back to your initial situation

In short: you think of your problem, tune into your physical body as it responds to your problem, you explore the underlying feeling and you offer the various keys to open your heart. Following this you recall your initial problem and notice any changes.

This sequence: problem – body – emotion – heart – problem, you repeat over and over until you are "through" with it. You are through when:

- you have discovered the pain underneath your problem and woken up out of your identification with it
- your physical body no longer tenses or displays any other unpleasant symptoms when you think of your initial situation
- your initial situation no longer triggers emotions that you identify with
- you have achieved a new perspective, more distance and more options of responding to the situation
- the situation no longer constitutes a problem for you.

Before getting started, please read the following explanations for each step.

Commentary on each step

The starting point: choose the topic and initial situation

Generally, you will sit down to practice the Keys to the Heart process because something has happened. Something that angers you, annoys or irritates you, throws you into despair, frightens or otherwise bothers you. Alternatively, you might be concerned about a situation in the future, something you are worried about or something you wish to be especially well prepared for. Therefore, when you sit down to do go through the Keys to the Heart process there is usually no need to look for the topic – it is already there. Unless, of course, you would like to practice for general "soul maintenance" purposes – which would be an excellent idea to do every morning.

In this case you do need to select a topic. This is usually not difficult, as there is always something that bothers you in some way – the situation you are in at present, something that happened recently or way back in your childhood, something that you are facing in your future, a challenging relationship, or even an event that you are looking forward to. Simply observe your thoughts for a while and find out which topic they circle around. Another method of selecting a topic is to imagine the fairy godmother visiting you with the offer to solve a problem for you. Which one would you choose?

There is also the possibility of starting with a purely physical symptom. This is always advisable when physical discomfort is at the forefront of your mind – as in case of a headache or back pain. Then the physical symptom lends itself as the natural entry point - allowing you to skip the step "topic" and go straight to body sensation. During the last step of the exercise, "back to the initial topic" you'd return to the part of the body where the physical symptom had manifested and observe any changes.

The initial situation

When you chose a topic, avoid staying general or abstract – choose instead an actual situation that you have experienced or are worried about experiencing. If, for example, you wanted to work on the topic *"women always dismiss me"*, remember a specific situation in which you felt that way. If your topic concerns anything that seems to *always* happen to you, or a way you *always* react, then please don't focus on the *always*, but pick one specific event in which this happened. This is your "initial situation" with which you start and end your session. Usually this is a situation that has already happened; sometimes the one you are in right now; or one that is yet to come.

Perceiving body sensations

Every emotion expresses itself through the physical body. When a situation triggers an emotion and you feel your emotion consciously, the physical sensation arising from it will eventually disappear. However, if you suppress your emotions as soon as you notice them - and repeat this over and over again - then an energy flow is blocked and something that should be in (e) *motion*, instead freezes. On the upside, these "frozen emotions" in the form of physical symptoms also offer you a simple means by which you can get back in touch with the feelings you have suppressed at any point you choose.

When you think of the situation you are struggling with, all emotions that you subconsciously connect to this situation are activated in your body. Most of these emotions stem from way back in your childhood and don't actually belong to the situation you are dealing with right now. In other words, these emotions are not *caused* by your present situation, but merely get triggered by it. They have been sitting in storage in your body and now make themselves known as a symptom or a specific body sensation. Perhaps you pull up your shoulders or your stomach is overcome by a feeling of anxiety and nausea. It is possible that your rigid shoulders are hiding a subconscious fear and the unpleasant jitter in your stomach might hide a fearful excitement. The nausea perhaps a subconscious disgust of something.

Discovering the emotion

When you immerse yourself with your whole attention in your bodily sensation and experience this sensation consciously and curiously, sooner or later you will become aware which emotion is hidden within it. This step – discovering the emotion contained in the bodily sensation – is actually made up of two parts. First, you discover the emotion and name it (e.g. *"I am dealing with fear here"*), and second, you actually feel the emotion you have discovered. This means that you tune into your breathing while at the same time concentrating on the feeling with the intent to experience it, explore it, get to know it.

Opening your heart to the emotion: trying out the keys to the heart

When your heart is open, you feel. When your heart is closed, you don't feel. Like the rest of us, you will most likely have closed your heart to a whole host of emotions.

Perhaps you have suppressed a certain longing in you because you assumed that its fulfilment was impossible. Perhaps you have kept your zest for life at bay so that you would not have to feel guilty for living. Perhaps you have forbidden yourself to feel hate, because you considered it as ridiculous, or as bad. Perhaps you have suppressed your fear because "scaredy-pants" were not tolerated in your family and you have taken on this tradition unquestioned.

The specific way you chose to suppress a feeling acts like a specific latch that locks the heart from this feeling. If you are to open your heart again, this latch needs to be removed, which is done by finding the correct key. Each of those keys represents the opposite of whatever you did to lock your feelings out of your heart. Rather than pondering long and hard over what exactly you might have done, an easy way is to simply try out each key and observe which one(s) you react to. The emotion of fear - as in the example above - might react to the key "understanding", the emotion hate might react to "permission to exist" or "being freed of judgement". The zest for life you have been suppressing might react to "being given room" or "to be recognised as a feeling as opposed to a fact" or perhaps even to "mercy". A suppressed longing might respond to "being considered possible".

The opening of the heart is something that happens all by itself, as soon as the right key is offered or even just thought of.

Here are the 10 most important Keys to the Heart:

1. being seen
2. acknowledgement
3. understanding
4. permission
5. compassion
6. mercy
7. respect
8. space
9. being felt
10. being recognised as a feeling as opposed to being considered a fact

Some keys have variations. It is important to find the exact words that your emotion responds to.

Here a list of the 10 Keys to the Heart with a few alternative formulations added:

1. **being seen**, being noticed
2. **acknowledgement**, recognising that this feeling exists as opposed to ignoring or denying it
3. **understanding** a feeling and recognising that it has a good reason to be there
4. **permission**, being given right to exist, being allowed to exist, being freed of judgement, rehabilitation
5. **compassion**, empathy,
6. **mercy**, to be with it, to take care of it rather than leaving it alone
7. **respect**, appreciation, esteem, high regard
8. **space**, room to exist, to spread, to be seen in its full magnitude
9. **being felt**, not just being noticed; feeling it with every cell of your body; allowing yourself to experience the feeling fully
10. **being recognised as a feeling as opposed to being considered a fact;** even if there is a fact, that which you actually watch is the way you *feel* about the fact.

Back to the initial topic / initial situation

In the beginning you were – without realising it – identified with a feeling. This coloured your point of view and your attitude in the initial situation. Now you have discovered your feeling, freed it from its lock-up in your physical body, and opened your heart to it.

The result will be that you will experience the same or similar situations in a completely new way. In order to prepare yourself for this, you can finish your session by once again vividly imagining your initial situation. You will notice that you can now calmly feel your newly discovered emotion, safe in the knowledge that it is "just" a feeling and not a fact.

The feeling is well settled within your own heart, you can feel it with respect or with whatever it needed from you. In this way you can now observe the situation and notice what has changed. How are you behaving now? How do you see the situation? How does it feel? Watch your inner film and memorize the result. This exercise will help you in a real situation to immediately notice your emotion and to consciously feel it, as opposed to identifying with it and falling back into your usual pattern of reaction.

Recognising when you have taken on other people's feelings and giving them back

On occasion you will discover feelings that don't even belong to you, but that you have taken on from another person. How do you recognise such feelings and get rid of them? By way of intuition, which will raise questions such as: *"Is this feeling actually mine?"* or *"Isn't this how my mother always felt when she...?"* Your intuition could pipe up at the very beginning, when you are just starting to notice a certain feeling, or it could put a thought into your head when you realise that none of the Keys to the Heart seem to be working. Or during the last step, when you are visualising your initial situation and notice that nothing has changed.

As soon as you suspect that a feeling might not actually be your own, do take this suspicion seriously. Don't second guess yourself or push the suspicion aside, or take it for the gospel – simply check whether it is true or not. And this is how you check it: Imagine giving the feeling in question back to that person and observe what happens in your inner image and in your emotional state. Sometimes the person might take it immediately, sometimes she refuses. In this case you might still feel that it belongs to her: in this case you can simply place it at her feet. Watch what this does to you. Feel better? Relieved? Touched? Maybe nothing changed, and you might ask yourself whether you made a mistake and gave it to the wrong person. Or is it indeed just your own feeling? To be on the safe side imagine all the people who are involved in your problem, and add your mother, father and other important people of your childhood (because most of the foreign feelings belong to our parents) as well as a figure that represents "unknown". Then offer the feeling to everyone and observe what happens in your inner film. Watch your own reaction: It's about you here, so what is important is not so much whether a person takes it or not, but how *you* feel afterwards. Relieved? Liberated? Completely or just a little? Or guilty, bad, sad ...? Do not just notice this new feeling, but feel it in your body and open your heart to it by checking the "keys".

Let's get started

Before starting with the Keys to the Heart process, please read through these more comprehensive instructions first, then put them aside. To remind yourself of the individual steps and the 10 Keys to the Heart during the process, please just use the two summary sheets provided on the next pages.

Detailed Instructions

Preparation:

Make sure that you won't be disturbed for at least half an hour.
Sit down upright and comfortably. Close your eyes.

Remind yourself what this exercise is all about: to shine the light of your consciousness onto the *feelings* that are behind your current issue and to open your heart to them. To be able to discover the feelings behind an issue, you will of course also have to look at the facts making up the issue, but please always remember that the facts are *not* the focus of this exercise, but only the feelings.

Switch on your conscious perception: by noticing your breathing, noticing your body and becoming aware of all your senses. Breath, body, sensory perceptions.

Select your topic and initial situation

Now choose the issue or topic that you want to look at.
Conjure up the initial situation vividly in your imagination.
As soon as the inner movie of your initial situation is rolling, press the stop button.

Become aware of the response of your physical body

Direct your attention to your physical body.
Notice your breathing.
Now guide your attention through your entire body from the top of your head to the bottom of your feet and find out whether you can notice anything unusual. Perhaps a burning, a shaking, a pain, a tension, a cramp, a numbness, a softening or hardening, heat or cold. Wherever you notice anything unusual, explore further with the intention to really get to know this particular body sensation. Immerse yourself completely into this part of your body, notice your breathing (without changing anything about it) and consciously experience your body sensations.

Discover the emotion

While experiencing your body sensations, tune in to how you are feeling. What emotion comes up? What emotion is being expressed through the body sensation and wants to gain attention? Don't *think* about it, but really feel how you are feeling while your entire attention is focused on experiencing this particular body sensation.

Perhaps you recognise and name the feeling immediately – fear, sadness, anger... Perhaps you need to tune in to the feeling for a while and consciously feel it while you are vividly imagining your initial situation, in order to be able to name it. If it's difficult, try to find an approximate description: *"I feel like someone who's been scolded"* or *"I feel like a loser"*.

Once you have discovered, recognised and named your feeling, dedicate some time to it. This feeling has been there for a long time and finally you have discovered it – so please take some time to consciously feel it. Feel your breath and say to yourself: *"For once I really want to consciously experience this feeling"*.

Sometimes you have to stay on the edge, so to speak: allow the feeling to its fullest extent, but knowing that it is a feeling. Not letting the feeling overwhelm you, but not letting it go away either. If it overwhelms you, bring your attention back to how it feels physically.

Remind yourself that you are looking at a feeling, not at a fact.

Open your heart to your feeling

Ask yourself the question
"What does this feeling need from my heart?"

In answer to your question, suggest the following 10 Keys to the Heart:

1. being seen
2. acknowledgement
3. understanding
4. permission
5. compassion
6. mercy
7. respect
8. space
9. being felt
10. being recognised as a feeling as opposed to being considered a fact.

Following are a few hints for testing your way through the different keys. Tune in to your breathing, feel the feeling consciously, ask yourself what this feeling (name it) needs from you but has never received before, and then offer in your mind or out loud a key and wait for a reaction. If you are experiencing a sense of agreement, relief or being shaken to the core, then the key fits. The latch, or at least one of the latches that locked a feeling out of your heart, has opened up.

It is however possible that your heart is barricaded with several latches and it is therefore useful to try out all keys and their different variations. Some feelings only require one key, some several and some all ten. It is also very useful to go through the ten keys a second time, as some keys only work after another latch has been removed. For example, the key "mercy" might not get any response during the first round, but once your feeling has received the "respect" it needed it might become quite receptive to mercy afterwards.

The point of this exercise is not to simply throw the whole key bundle at your buried feelings saying: *"here, you've got everything you might need"*, but to find out *what exactly* your feelings need by consciously feeling them and offering the keys one by one. Your heart will open all by itself when the correct key is offered and you recognise the opening by your reaction.

Now your heart has opened up to your feeling and you have a different relationship to it. At the beginning your feeling possessed you, dominated you, you disappeared within it. Now YOU are present and are merely experiencing the feeling.

Your feeling is smaller than you and it lives in your heart. You are now in a position to look at the situation unperturbed by the feeling.

Back to the topic and initial situation

This is the last step. Think of your initial situation and immerse yourself in it – the same situation that you started this journey on. It's just that now - different to before - you are consciously aware of your feelings. You don't try to shove them under the carpet, you are not compensating for them, nor are you actively expressing your feelings – you simply observe that you are having this feeling during this situation.

What has changed? Your view of the situation? Your attitude? Your body sensation? How would you act now? Mentally take note of this feeling and set the intention to notice it, should it be triggered again by something in the future.

If nothing has changed...

Please note: There are occasions when little or nothing happens when doing this exercise. Either you already notice while trying out the ten keys that none of them really seem to fit, or you notice during the last step, when you are revisiting your initial situation. In this case there are two possible explanations:

a) You are still identified with the feeling. You haven't actually consciously perceived the feeling, but are still identified with it. The solution: shift your attention 180 degrees by directing it away from the situation and towards yourself: your body sensations and the associated feelings. Remind yourself that this exercise is *not* about the situation, but the feelings it triggers in you. Consciously leave the situation aside for the moment – you can always come back to it later.

b) The feeling is not yours. The feeling that you have tried to open your heart to turns out to not belong there at all, because it belongs to another person. You might have picked this feeling up from a person you encountered recently or you've been carrying it around for ages, after picking it up as a child from your parents or other authority figures. The solution: if the exercise doesn't really seem to work, ask yourself: *"who does this feeling belong to, or who could I have picked this up from?"*. Work with the pictures and hunches that come up and do not doubt them.

Imagine the person(s) involved and hand the feeling back as if it were an object. Say in your mind or out loud something along the lines of: *"I have this anger here, and somehow, I got the impression that I took it on from you. I hereby hand it back."* Watch what happens in your inner movie. Sometimes it all goes without a hitch and you feel relieved and liberated. Sometimes a new feeling comes up that prevents you from completing the return. You can take care of this by working through the steps of the Keys to the Heart process once more: i.e., where in my body is this feeling lodged? What does it feel like? What does it take for my heart to open up to it? Is this perhaps another feeling that I need to return to sender?

If a good feeling arises, don't just stay identified with it ("I am free") as if this were your new reality but remember that this work is about perceiving feelings instead of staying identified with them! Feel it consciously and open your heart to it. Note its name on a paper, memorise the feeling and the corresponding body state and make a resolution to take care of it by feeling it again and again until it takes root in your heart.

Then go back to your initial situation and see what has changed. Should yet another feeling crop up, go through the steps again and find it a place in your heart or return to sender. Make a mental note of this feeling or write it down and set the intention to keep an eye on it in future situations.

Take a deep breath in and then breathe out with a sigh.

Open your eyes.

Write down a few key words to remember your initial situation and the name of the feeling that you either let into your heart or returned to sender.

On the next pages you find a short overview that helps you to memorize the process, an example to illustrate the procedure, and then two summaries that will help you to go through the process. You can use these as a cheat sheet while you practice, while the exercise is still new to you. Later you won't need it anymore, because you will have internalized the steps and their meaning.

Later, you will be able to apply the exercise in your daily life without having to retreat especially for it. For this, however, it is important that you have first tried several times in dry run.

If you practice consistently for a while, this will happen automatically afterwards. This will save you a lot of problems.

Recap the steps in short (to read through before commencing the exercise)

1. **switch on the light** – you switch on conscious perception
2. **choose a topic** – you select a topic you want to work on
3. **body sensations** – you notice what sensations your topic triggers in your body and experience these sensations consciously
4. **discover feeling** – you notice any feelings behind the body sensation
5. **open heart** – you check through the ten Keys to the Heart and check which one(s) unlock(s) your heart to your feeling
6. **return to sender** (where applicable) – you ask yourself whether you have taken on the feeling from someone else and if yes, return it
7. **revisit initial situation** – you visualise your initial situation and observe any changes
8. **completion** – you take note of the feeling you worked with and set the intention to keep an eye on it if it should get triggered again.

Here is a short example to illustrate the process, including returning a feeling:

Example: Carlos and the green-eyed monster

Carlos is annoyed with Paul, his colleague from the office. Whenever Carlos wants to shine with one of his successes, Paul tries to trump him with one of his own stories. Working through the steps Carlos notices tension in his stomach area and identifies anger as the associated feeling. He tries out all ten Keys to the Heart, but none of them really move him. Then it hits him that the anger might not be his own, but Paul's. In his mind Carlos returns the anger to Paul and he feels immediately lighter. Where he felt anger before, Carlos now understands that it was Paul who was angry with him because he was jealous.

On the following pages you'll find two summaries that you can use to guide you through the process.

The steps – briefly sketched

- switch on conscious perception
- choose topic and initial situation
- tune in to your body
- discover feeling, name it, really feel it
- test through the 10 keys
- revisit initial situation and notice changes
- where applicable, return other people's feelings

The 10 Keys – Short form to memorize

1. being noticed, being seen
2. acknowledging that this feeling exists
3. understanding
4. permission to exist, being freed of judgement
5. compassion, empathy
6. mercy, to take care of it
7. respect, appreciation, esteem, high regard
8. space, to be seen in its full magnitude
9. feeling it with every cell of your body
10. recognise it as a feeling as opposed to a fact

Extra key for the feeling of **longing** or **nostalgia**: to be freed from the idea of impossibility (= considering the fulfilment of your longing possible) Extra key for **positive feelings**: care, to feel it often, to remember this feeling.

What happens next?

Now you have been introduced to the basic exercise of the Keys to the Heart process and have taken a first step towards finding a solution to your problem. Even this first step – to become consciously aware of a feeling that sits just below the surface – can result in noticeable change.

Example: I am afraid of my landlord

My landlord calls a meeting and I am dreading it. This man always comes across to me as so intimidating! I close my eyes, direct my full attention towards my fear and open my heart to it. Suddenly the landlord does not appear to be so big and scary any more. When we finally meet, I experience him for the first time as friendly.

How to access the pain hidden behind a problem?

With the basic exercise the aim is to identify a feeling and open your heart to it. However, a problem is generally made up of several different feelings – negative, positive and neutral ones. And as explained earlier, the problem is based on a pain.

So how can you access this pain? Basically, there are two avenues:

Path One: Step-by-step

This means that you repeat the same steps as described above over and over again until the pain reveals itself. What a pain usually needs most of all is the following three keys: 1) to be noticed, 2) to be felt and 3) to be recognised as a feeling (because this is the very thing that has been missing so far). On occasion it also needs one of the other keys, so it is always useful to test through the entire key bundle.

Example: Jenny all alone

Jenny is distraught. Her boyfriend has left her and she has decided to use this as the initial situation for a Keys to the Heart session. In her throat she feels desperation and she opens her heart to this feeling using the keys of mercy, acknowledgement, permission and understanding. The key that has the most impact is recognising desperation as a feeling as opposed to a fact.

After this she discovers more feelings: anger, powerlessness, sadness, and finally the painful feeling - yet she is not sure whether it is loss or feeling abandoned that hurts so much. Jenny realises that most of all she feels abandoned. She really struggles applying the key "recognizing it as a feeling" – is it not a fact that she was abandoned?! Yet then it dawns on her that she is dealing with two separate things: a fact – out there, and a feeling – in here. And this feeling in here wants to be recognised as such, wants to find a place in her heart and wants to be felt with every cell of her body. The other keys don't even come into play anymore. Jenny realises that this feeling has always been with her since she was a little girl and her mother died. Back then it was impossible to feel it, as everything was just so bad, and nobody with an open heart was there for her, to encourage her to feel her feelings, so she had locked her heart.

Jenny realises that this new situation with her boyfriend is actually an opportunity for her to heal her wounded soul, because this is what is actually happening through her exercise: healing. It feels like coming home, as if a part of herself that she had banished is now allowed home. She feels good. somehow comforted, and even though the outer circumstances are exactly the same, they just

don't feel as bad anymore, because she is now present to herself and no longer abandoned.

Path Two to the pain underneath the problem: the shortcut

There is a shortcut, but it comes with a warning at the outset that it doesn't work in every situation. You can always give it a go, but as soon as you realise that it is not working because feelings other than you are expecting are cropping up, revert back to path 1: open your heart to the feelings in the order they present themselves via your body sensations. Avoid forcing a breakthrough – sometimes there are just too many emotions that want to be acknowledged first. Some of them are too important to be looked at for a moment and then immediately left behind in order to discover the next feeling.

Here 's the shortcut – it too has two variations:

Variation 1: Interviewing the negative emotion

Explanations with two examples follow immediately;

Variation 2: Experiencing the initial situation unguarded

Explanations illustrated by an example on the following pages.

Shortcut – Variation 1: Interviewing the negative emotion

Once you have brought the feeling close to the surface into your heart, which is generally a negative emotion, you can interview this emotion, asking it how it came about and what it is in relation to. How come I am feeling this anger? What is so bad that it can make me so angry? What is going on with me right now? What is so bad that I feel desperate?

Consciously listen to the answers and allow the pain that expresses itself through them to reveal itself. Make a point of staying in the mode "conscious awareness" and remind yourself that you are dealing with a feeling and not a fact. Invite the pain to show itself to you while you are actively noticing your breath. Really get to know this pain. It is a feeling and like every other feeling it wants nothing more than finally to be seen and allowed to come home into your heart.

Sometimes this works straight away, and the pain that had been suppressed for so long, because subconsciously you mistook it for a fact, reveals itself.

In this case, stay in the conscious position, allow yourself to feel this pain and open your heart to it.

Example: Triggers from childhood

Lou is having a fight with her husband. Nothing overly dramatic happens, but when her husband suddenly gets up and leaves the room in the middle of their argument, Lou bursts into tears.

She is feeling desperate, really desperate. Lou realizes that her desperation is completely out of proportion to the silly little thing they started arguing about and asks herself what could have made her feels like this... The response is another outburst of tears. She feels deserted, and this feeling is extremely painful for her. Lou remembers feeling this way as a child and has a sudden realization: her desperation today has nothing to do with her husband leaving the room, but because it brought an old pain from her childhood to the surface that she hadn't been consciously aware of before.

In other cases, it doesn't work quite as smoothly, because another emotion that wants to be seen first, pushes into the foreground. Sometimes it is a fear, that the underlying pain is just too much, or a rage, or an evasive reaction such as: *"Suddenly I can't feel a thing any more, everything has gone blank!"*. The only thing to do here is: To go on working step by step. Open your heart to every feeling that shows up in your body, until you are ready to open your heart to the pain that lies underneath.

Example: Jonas and the pain of loss

Jonas has joined my seminar to deal with a very painful event in his life. His wife left him a year ago and he still hasn't got over it. As he is talking about it, he is very nervous, fidgeting with his hands; his eyes are clouded in darkness and we can feel his great pain. Yet as he starts the Keys to the Heart process and concentrates on his physical body, he somehow can't detect any reaction whatsoever. When asked how it feels to remember the separation from his wife he answers: "Good". He reports that his body feels totally relaxed and that he can't detect a single negative symptom. "Great", I say, "then please now consciously perceive this positive bodily sensation – how do you feel in it?" "Relaxed", says Jonas, "in peace somehow". I ask him to fully open his heart for this feeling of relaxation and peace. It needs room and permission to exist. At this point I suggest to Jonas to bring the session to a close in order to really allow this feeling room, but he wants to carry on. He desperately wants to get to the core of the issue. When he again reminds himself of the separation from his wife, he indeed notices a symptom in his body: great restlessness. He becomes fidgety, his hands and feet start twitching and his whole body becomes uneasy. "How do you feel with this body sensation?", I ask. "Restless – in fact I can't bear thinking about it!" replies Jonas. "Could you call this feeling "Can't bear it" or "Unbearable"? "Yes, exactly! Unbearable!" Jonas proceeds to open his heart to this unbearable feeling. "What exactly is it that you can't bear?", I ask. This question makes Jonas experience a severe pain shooting into his consciousness: "To have lost her", he says and bursts into tears. It takes Jonas a while to realize that now he is not dealing with the fact of her loss, but with the feeling of it. When he finally manages to open his heart to the pain of losing his wife, his state suddenly changes dramatically. The pain needed acknowledgement, permission to exist, room, and being recognized as a feeling as opposed to a fact. After applying these keys Jonas says: "Strange – when I recognize this pain as a feeling and give it room and acceptance, I suddenly feel connected to my wife, no matter whether we are together or apart. And this connection doesn't even wane when

I imagine her living with somebody else, or on a another continent, or even if she was dead".

I invite Jonas to consciously perceive this new, wonderful feeling too, and to give it a space in his heart. "Now it feels complete", he says. "I feel ready to start a new chapter in my life.

Shortcut – Variation 2: Experiencing the initial situation unguarded

You have taken a negative emotion into your heart and given it everything it needed. Now you want to find out what the underlying pain of this negative emotion is. The technique: you let your emotion know that – for the purpose of this exercise - you would like to set it aside for a moment. Afterwards it is of course allowed back into your heart. In your mind you now tune in to your initial situation, but this time without guarding yourself with the help of your negative emotion. You put all negative emotions to one side, you don't protect yourself with defiance or anger, you don't block anything with fear, you don't run anywhere or try to disappear in a flood of tears – in other words you are entering the situation with all your shields down. Reassure yourself that this is not about doing this in real life, but just in your imagination for the purpose of coaxing out the pain hiding underneath your surface feelings. If you are lucky, or if you just happen to be ready for this, the pain will show itself

Example: Outraged

Anger. Rage. How dares this guy?!

I feel tempted to scream at him or hit him in the face...

OK. I close my eyes and look at my rage. I am huffing and puffing when breathing. Flared nostrils. Arms, jaw, belly, legs – my whole body feels tense. So angry! Breathe. Feel. Open my heart to this anger. It needs the whole lot: to become consciously aware of it, to really feel it, to be acknowledged, to be understood, allowed to exist, respected, and to be recognised as a feeling.

Finally it settles, it no longer seems larger than me, like something that has taken me over. Now it is smaller than me and lives in my heart.

What on earth has made me so angry??? What is causing me that much pain?

In order to find out I imagine experiencing the same situation again, just this time minus the anger. I enter the situation without the tension of anger and the outrage that is bubbling up, I tell it: "Yes, I can see you, and you are definitely allowed into my heart, but right now, would you please just step aside for one moment". Now I allow the behaviour of this guy to impact on me fully, without shield or defences. How does this make me feel?

Belittled. Humiliated.

This is it. The terrible feeling, the pain I was so afraid of, because I mistook it for a fact.

I get to know this feeling, allow it, feel it and open my heart to it. After that, the incident that just a moment ago made me livid with anger doesn't even get a rise out of me anymore. I realise that the guy simply is the way he is and that this has nothing to do with me.

Wherever there is a problem, there is a longing

Every problem also has some kind of longing associated with it that we are commonly not aware of.

Every pain is connected to a longing. Usually this longing is completely suppressed, because your attention always focused on whatever angered, annoyed, scared or saddened you, and not on whatever you'd rather have.

This longing – usually the opposite of your pain – can show itself at various stages of the process. Either when you are just about to discover the hidden pain, or at the very beginning of the exercise, or anywhere in between. Whenever you notice a longing, stop your inner movie and direct your full attention towards it.

"If only...", *"I wish I had..."*, *"But I want..."* or *"I so long for..."* are all hints that you are harbouring a longing that wants to show itself. Put your longing into the most simple and precise words you can think of and tune in to your body. What does it feel like to long for this? Where do you feel this longing? And what does this longing need from your heart? Test your way through all the keys and then test another very important one that only applies to longings: *"to be freed from the thought of impossibility"* or expressed the other way round *"to be thought of as being possible"*. This key is important because we often push longings aside simply because we don't believe that it's even possible for them to come true. However, a longing is a feeling – YOUR feeling - and like any other feeling it doesn't like being suppressed. It simply wants to be consciously felt and find a place in your heart.

By the way, when applying the "impossibility"-key to a longing, it is *not* about making a point that the fulfilment of your longing is indeed possible, but about checking whether removing the impossibility-lid from your longing brings you relief - whether it gets a reaction from your heart that indicates that this is what your longing needed. So please don't violate your mind by convincing it that something is possible, but simply *feel* your longing, ask it what it needs and observe whether to be considered possible triggers a reaction. That's all. The lid is removed. Your longing is allowed to live within you and you will notice that this in and of itself is a huge shift. The energy can flow more freely in you, you can breathe more deeply, you can look into the future with confidence, even if your head has no idea why and how. Sometimes your heart is simply wiser than your head...

The hidden treasure under your problems: the positive feeling underneath a longing

If you want to, you can go one step further. Because just as all negative emotions hide an underlying pain, all longings contain the hidden treasure of a positive emotion.

The pathway: ask yourself what the fulfilment of your longing would look like in concrete terms. Whenever there is a longing or a wish (a longing is basically the feeling belonging to a wish), there is also an image of its fulfilment. Discover this image. If you are longing for freedom, what does this freedom look like? What do you see yourself doing or experiencing? Really tune into this image, just as you have tuned into your initial situation. Now walk through the steps of the exercise: body-feeling-heart. What is happening in your body; what does it feel like to be in this desired situation? Experience your body sensations consciously and attentively. What is the feeling called? Give it a name that describes it as accurately as possible and then open your heart to it by offering it each of the 10 keys, except "mercy" and "compassion". Add the additional key of care – which means that positive feelings don't just want to be brushed off by noticing them for a few seconds, but that they may want to be felt often and deeply in order to feel truly welcomed in your heart.

How many layers do problems consist of and how do we know that we have worked our way through them all?

Basically, you are through with a problem when it no longer constitutes a problem for you! Usually this happens after you have opened your heart to a pain. However, sometimes the discovery of a positive feeling underneath a longing seems to result in even bigger changes. In other cases, the pain doesn't seem to be the core of an issue, because a surface feeling was much more important. For example, you might have easily identified the pain of being betrayed, yet gone through a huge process to feel the anger about the betrayal, because you have never before allowed yourself to feel anger. In other cases still, the freeing change occurs when you realise that you have taken on a feeling, or bundle of feelings, from someone else and given it back. Some problems are based not only on one pain but on several! If this is your case you will not have solved the problem until you have taken care of them all. Example: Someone criticizes you and you find this humiliating. After opening your heart to this feeling of humiliation, you realize that it is still a drama for you. Eventually you discover a second basic pain: that of injustice.

Or you've been abandoned in your childhood, and this left a number of psychological wounds in your psyche, depending on how you interpreted the facts at that time. So you suffer from the pain of feeling abandoned, worthless, bad (if he/she leaves me, I must be a bad person), betrayed, ugly ...

Anyway, you are through with the problem as soon as you have discovered the pain(s) at the bottom of this problem, and woke up from the identification with this feeling(s).

In every problem you find several layers of emotion:

- Negative emotions (they help you not feel the pain), like anger, sadness, fear.
- Positive or neutral emotions (which you can also use for repressing the pain), like peace, detachment
- Pain (that which hurts you) (= the core of the problem)
- Longing for the opposite (for instance, longing for acceptance when your pain is that of feeling rejected).
- Beautiful feeling (which is to be found in the fulfilment of this longing) (eventually the deepest layer waiting to be discovered).

This overview can serve you as a kind of road map. Don't use it as a working plan because you cannot work through your problem following a logical plan. The psyche has its own logic. Feelings show up when it is time for them to show up.

Therefore, instead of saying "today I want to explore layer No. 2" simply start every session or every new step by looking into your body. Take the feelings as they arise in your body.

Some issues are dealt with quickly and others take more time!

It is close to impossible to work through each of your problems according to some logical plan, because your psyche simply does not follow the same logic as your brain. One day everything goes nicely to plan: negative emotion 1, negative emotion 2, underlying pain, longing, positive emotion... on another day nothing seems to be working. In this case take pause and check what it feels like when nothing works. One day the pain shows itself at the very beginning and no further work is necessary; another day it could happen that the process starts with a longing and that you get stuck on an emotion - could this emotion perhaps belong to someone else? Be prepared for anything. As long as you stay in conscious perception mode, nothing bad can happen. You'll simply find that some topics you can work through faster and others will take a bit longer! All you need to remember in the back of your mind is the basic steps of the Keys to the Heart process and a map of emotions that can come up.

On the next page you will find an overview of the steps and the different levels of feelings.

The basic steps:

- Topic
- Body
- Emotion
- Heart
- Topic
- Return to sender (optional)

The different layers of emotions that can be part of a problem or topic:

- negative emotion (which you use to avoid pain)
- positive or neutral emotions (which you also sometimes use to avoid pain)
- pain (the thing that really bothers you)
- longing (for the opposite of the pain)
- lovely feeling (associated with the fulfilment of your longing)

Example: Dignified Charlie

*Charlie is upset with his girlfriend because she has ridiculed him in front of his friends (*initial situation*).*

When he sits down to look at it, he is able to vividly recall the initial situation, but somehow the anger has gone. Instead, Charlie feels quite serene, as if he is above it all. He opens his *heart to this feeling of serenity (*a positive feeling*) and what it needs is permission and acknowledgement, and that it is recognised as a feeling as opposed to a fact — i.e., even though he momentarily feels serene, this is not necessarily his new reality. As soon as he applies this last key, he can feel the anger bubble up in his stomach (*negative emotion*). Going through the keys, he finds that his heart opens to the anger with understanding and respect. Finally, he realises why he felt so angry: he felt humiliated (*underlying pain*). Once he allows himself to feel this feeling of humiliation and recognise it as a feeling, he returns to the initial situation in his mind's eye. How would he experience this situation if it happened again? He consciously feels the feeling of humiliation while he runs through the scene in his imagination. It feels different. He feels much more centred, at one with himself and looking out for himself. He realises that the thoughts and feelings of the others are none of his business. The whole scenario doesn't bother him so much anymore and Charlie notices that his posture has changed: more upright and taller. He tunes in to this body sensation and discovers a new feeling: dignity (*lovely feeling*). He opens his heart for this feeling too.*

With this feeling of dignity in his heart he can imagine telling his girlfriend that her behaviour has hurt him. However, it doesn't seem all that important anymore, as he has realised that dignity is a feeling and nobody can take this from him. He just has to remember to feel it again whenever the need arises.

In this example the different layers of feelings appear in a relatively logical order. Initially there is anger, which is pushed aside by the sudden attitude *"I can rise above this"*. Only after this has found a place in Charlie's heart, do the anger and the underlying pain dare to show themselves. During the revisiting of the initial situation, another positive feeling appears. Yet it could have all happened in a completely different order. Simply deal with each feeling as it appears and look after them without getting hung up on any particular order. If you are just about to discover a pain, and fear pushes in, then simply deal with the fear first. If you are just working on anger, and despair appears out of nowhere, then turn your attention to the despair. The basic principle is to always deal with what is right in front of you. Where can you feel it in your body? What does it feel like? What does it need from your heart? If you stay consciously aware, the pain at the core of the issue will inevitably reveal itself.

The order of the steps of the exercise can also vary. Normally you start with the topic, go to the body sensation and then the emotion, but sometimes, as in the above example, the emotion is already clear to you.

Then of course the body sensation comes after the emotion instead of before. If you are angry, ask yourself: *"Where in my body does this anger sit?"* or *"How do I experience this anger physically?"*. You only truly feel your anger once you have become aware of your associated body sensations. Therefore, please never skip the body sensation step! And please always consciously notice your breathing.

The role of breathing

Don't attempt to change your breathing in any way, but simply become aware of it in relation to your situation or emotion. With some emotions your breath will become shallow, with others you will breathe heavily and with others still you might breathe deeply and calmly, or even feel as if you've stopped breathing. Please do not correct anything – the intention is not to breathe the feeling "away" but to use the breath to feel your feeling more clearly and fully.

Sometimes you may even feel like crying while an emotion surfaces. This is quite all right, but please be mindful not to cry yourself into state where you are identifying with your emotion (the emotion = you), but always remain the observer of the emotion you are experiencing. Consciously perceive your crying and the feeling that is expressed therein. Remember: you are not the sad one, but the one noticing and experiencing the feeling of sadness and the one who is taking care of it.

The following example illustrates a successful (even though sometimes tough) Keys to the Heart session.

Example: Bea moves on

Background: *Bea has lost her husband and now, after years of mourning, wants to start a new life. However, she still clings to the past quite a bit and wants to work on that.*

Initial situation: *Bea recently met a really nice and interesting man, yet instead of chatting to him casually or perhaps even flirting with him a bit (which she would have liked to), she somehow started feeling guilty and left rather hastily. She uses the image of her rushed exit as her initial situation.*

Body: *She literally feels torn apart – like one locomotive pulling her backwards from behind and another locomotive pulling her forwards from the front.*

Feeling: *torn, pulled in two different directions.*

Keys to her heart: *conscious noticing, acknowledgement, space.*

Further discoveries: *Bea focuses on the locomotive pulling her backwards. The associated feeling is retreating, running away – actually: fear. She asks herself what she is afraid of. It's about losing something if she allows herself to enter a new relationship. To lose her husband completely. She opens her heart to this fear with understanding, respect, acknowledgement, noticing.*

The locomotive pulling her forward brings up a longing – the longing to get to know this new man. She opens her heart to this longing – it mainly needs freeing from judgement, and respect. Then she suddenly has a hunch: could this longing she feels actually be more his feeling than hers? She imagines handing it back to this man, and he accepts it and she feels lighter and less under pressure.

At the same time, she notices a feeling of joy – realising that he longs for her as much as she does for him – and this feeling of joy too is offered a place in her heart. It wants to be felt, receive permission to exist and space.

Bea wants to bring her session to a close, yet something draws her back to the fear that she discovered at the beginning of the exercise. The fear that she will lose her husband forever if she enters a new relationship. She notices that another feeling is hiding underneath this fear – a pain. Perhaps she should open her heart to this feeling too? But this would mean imagining the dreaded outcome. As best as she is able to, Bea imagines what it feels like losing her husband completely. Her last connection to him – her mourning, her loneliness, her keeping him in her thoughts – is over and she imagines him completely gone. What does this feel like? She feels emptiness – as if something is missing, something crucial. There are no clear body sensations – just the feeling of emptiness within her and around her. She concentrates on her physical body to find out how she feels about this emptiness, the missing. A severe pain surfaces in her heart and its name is "loss".

Bea initially struggles with feeling the pain of loss – it feels too bad, too much. It is as if by feeling it, she would make the loss a fact that is set in concrete. Then she reminds herself that at this moment she is not dealing with a fact, but with a feeling, and that this feeling needs her. It needs her to take mercy on it, to open her heart to it. Now she can feel the pain of loss.

It comes as a surprise to her, that besides wanting to be truly felt for once, the pain reacts most strongly to the key "being recognised as a feeling, as opposed to a fact". Then it also needs room, respect and acknowledgement. After this last key Bea realises that in reality there is no such thing as loss. Even though she can't explain it to her mind, she can feel it clearly in her heart. A new feeling has appeared: oneness. With this oneness in her heart and a feeling of joy, Bea is now in a position to contact her new acquaintance again. Luckily, she has his phone number...

Chapter Five

What can you achieve through the Keys to the Heart process?

Since I discovered this path,
I know that everything reveals its solution
when I just sit and watch
with patience and interest
and open my heart to whatever I find.
Sometimes it takes me deeply into the mysteries
of the human heart,
makes me understand myself, the others, the
situation.
Every step on this path makes me discover a
new perspective,
a new way of feeling, of being.

A method you can apply to any issue

Most problems dissolve of their own accord after being looked at with this method. This is because in most cases the problem is not the outer situation, but the way you have interpreted it and the feelings this interpretation has triggered within you. Once you drop your interpretation, those feelings are no longer triggered and the situation is simply a situation you have to deal with somehow - with the advantage of it no longer being a problem or a drama. Often you even come to realise that it was never a problem in the first place.

But in some cases, one is indeed faced with grave circumstances, where we can justifiably talk about a difficult problem "out there "- such as your partner leaving you, you losing your job or being attacked, or a loved one is gravely ill, or your credit card is blocked. In such cases the Keys to the Heart process can also help, even though of course, it can't alter the outer circumstances. How can it help then?

1. I am centred within myself (instead of being beside myself). This in itself is highly valuable. My attention is no longer captured by outer circumstances, but focused on myself, my body, my feelings. I no longer desert myself to

disappear in panic, powerlessness or anger; I am there for my feelings and I take care of them.

2. In this way I gain distance to the outer circumstances and other people.

3. Emotions no longer obscure my view of the situation. I can now see aspects and opportunities that have eluded me before. This also might foster intuition.

4. Consciously perceiving my feelings - even if just for a second - gives me a pause between the outer situation and my reaction to it. This pause is exactly the moment I need to go within and to know what to do.

5. Most importantly, I discover that however bad the outer situation is, I am more than my feelings, more than my thoughts, more than my body sensations. I am in touch with the part of me that is not entangled with people or situations, but simply observes. In spiritual traditions this part is called the witness, the observer or consciousness. This part is like an inner platform, on which even in dangerous situations I can find some form of inner security.

6. Because I am feeling my feelings, my heart is open. And if my heart is open, I can also feel what others are feeling. Apart from giving me

more understanding for them, this also offers me another advantage: when I know what others are feeling, I can interact with them more wisely.

Many situations we work on with the Keys to the Heart process are comparatively harmless on the level of the facts. This does not exclude, however, that emotionally they can feel like catastrophes. It only feels like a catastrophe because we mistake an emotion from the past for a fact in the present and therefore refuse to feel it. This unfortunate mix-up can completely dissolve through the Key to the Heart process.

However, we should not underestimate the fact that we do get deeply conditioned by the circumstances in our family of origin, the behaviours of our parents and our early childhood experiences. Thus, even with a lot of practising the Keys to the Heart process, it can sometimes still be challenging to free ourselves from this conditioning. Yet it is possible. With a lot of patience and conscious awareness we can release old patterns and become a new person.

Relatives usually tend towards wanting to push you back into your old role. They don't do this out of menace, but because they don't recognise you anymore, and this can be scary. Hence it is quite common to revert to old behaviour patterns when you are with family or old friends. You thought you had become this new person, self-confident and strong, yet in the presence of your relatives you can't help behaving like the little idiot that they have always accused you of being. This is normal. Simply stay present: this real-life situation offers you the opportunity to consciously feel the old feeling and find out what it might still need from your heart or who you have taken it on from.

The Keys to the Heart process does not actually turn you into a new person, it uncovers the person you've always been underneath the armour of your persona.

Moreover, each session has a way of turning out totally differently from what you imagined. For example, if you have always suffered from being too soft and relenting, you might imagine that after a Keys to the Heart session you are finally able to slam your fist on the table and tell people what's what. In actual fact, the session might result in you gaining so much inner strength and authority, or your heart might start beaming so impressively, that there is no need for fist slamming anymore, because people respect you automatically.

If your problem was that you always judged yourself harshly for dreaming away the day and being too lazy, you might imagine that as the result of your Keys to the Heart session you will roll up your sleeves and get stuck into things. Yet the session turns out unexpectedly: underneath your idleness you discover the feelings of being relaxed and non-attached and you can suddenly appreciate these feelings as a resource. Contrary to others who dread big projects, you have always been able to complete them with minimum effort and maximum efficiency.

So, the result of a successful Keys to the Heart session is usually surprising and much more satisfying than you initially imagined.

Practising the Keys to the Heart process usually solves problems completely. Even if a challenging situation "out there "remains, you have gained some distance from it, more clarity, more perspectives and new qualities through the exercise, that will help you deal with your challenges differently. You might for example discover your capacity to take action on something, after you recognise "feeling paralysed "as a feeling as opposed to a fact, and offer this feeling a place in your heart. Alternatively, a session might help you find the right words where you had none before – there are literally infinite possibilities of how body and feeling awareness can positively impact on a situation.

Some examples of what you can achieve through the Keys to the Heart process

- Getting to the bottom of problems and solving them
- Finding the right decision
- Healing old emotional wounds
- Awakening from false beliefs
- Getting rid of reaction and behaviour patterns
- Clarify and harmonise relationships
- Overcoming fears
- Learning to feel again
- Alleviate and heal physical symptoms
- Finding more self-love and inner security
- Understanding the feelings of others
- Opening your heart

- Ending conflicts or making them superfluous

- Developing Emotional Stability

- Finding a higher perspective

- Coming to serenity

- Initiate and support spiritual awakening

- Getting rid of extraneous burdens you have put on yourself

- How the Keys to the Heart Process can help you fulfil your longings

Getting to the bottom of problems and solving them

Most problems can be resolved by the Keys to the Heart Method. Because, as explained, the real problem is mostly not the outer situation but what it does to you on the emotional level.

But what if you are dealing with really serious external circumstances? I mean, materially, physically, factually and not only emotionally stressful? Like being dismissed, physically attacked, or your partner's dying, your credit card's been cancelled...

Can Keys to the Heart help there? It can't change the circumstances, can it?

What it always changes is how you feel with the situation, how you think about it, it helps you discover other possibilities of action, other perspectives, Depending on the situation, you will have more courage or presence, more insight and understanding, more calmness, serenity.

In many cases, even the outer situation changes as a result. Don't forget that we are connected to the world around us in many ways, many of which we are not aware of. Try it out!

But regardless of the question of whether Keys to the Heart will change the external situation or not, your feelings need your attention and care. They need your heart. This attention will make you feel better, regardless of the external situation.

You will be more with yourself (you will realise that you didn't even know that you were beside yourself before).

If there are feelings of panic, faintness or anger, you will not drown in them but be with them and take care of them like a mother of her child.

This provides you a healthy distance from circumstances and people.

Your emotions no longer block your perception of the situation.

You might perceive aspects or opportunities that you didn't see before.

Being aware of your feelings, even if it is only for seconds, provides you a buffer between the external situation and your reaction. Exactly what it needs in order to realise what you have to do.

Finally - the most important thing – you will discover: As bad as the situation may be, you are more than your feelings, more than your thoughts, more than your bodily sensations. Because by practicing this method you discover a part of yourself that is not entangled and involved, but simply perceives neutrally. In spiritual traditions this central part of ourselves is called "the witness", "the observer" or "the awareness". It is like an inner platform on which even in de facto dangerous situations, you can find a kind of inner security.

Another advantage: Since you are awake and have opened your heart you will be able to perceive the feelings of the persons who are involved in the situation with you, the emotions of your counterpart. This will protect you from taking over these feelings (which we normally do without realising it!). this also gives you the advantage of recognising how the other person feels. On one hand you will develop understanding for the person, on the other hand you will be able to deal with her more wisely.

But the vast majority of situations that we look at with the Keys to the Heart Method are on the level of facts - compared to a bomb attack or a financial or physical ruin - rather harmless. But emotionally they can be experienced as so disastrous that we are even able to kill ourselves our others because of them.

Yet, since in such cases the catastrophe consists only in the fact that we take an emotion from the past for a fact in the present, these problems completely dissolve when this confusion is uncovered through the Keys to the Heart process.

As I said, sometimes it is easy and fast, sometimes it needs patience. Childhood experiences, family and society have a profound effect on us which is deeply engraved in our brain. Through correct perception, opening your heart and giving back those emotions that do not belong to you, you can clear every problem. But the patterns that the past engraved in your brain are a reality on the physical level. They will make you react again and again in the old way. So, if you had a wonderful session with a great inner transformation, don't think that this is it. It is consistent continued practice in daily life situations that will truly free you and make you a new person. If you have discovered a basic pain in a session, make a resolution to keep an eye on it, to notice it as soon as it appears again, and then immediately recognise it as a feeling (instead of taking it for a fact as you unconsciously did before)! And if at the end of a session you have discovered a new positive feeling, nurture it by reminding yourself of it again and again!

This will make you behave in a new way. And through repeated new behaviour you override the old rails in the brain.

But beware of relapse: Relatives and friends might tend to push you back into your old role.

Not in order to harm you, but they are afraid not to recognise you. If you change it is as if they lose you. Maybe they feel obliged to respond to your change which they absolutely do not want. Even if the old role-play was rather unpleasant, they might feel more comfortable with it than with your new attitude.

And what is more, encountering these people automatically activates the old mechanisms in your brain. If you stay awake, you might just watch this without identifying with it. But normally we tend to fall back into an old behavioural pattern if we meet our family or an old circle of friends again. Even though having experienced yourself as a new person after the Keys to the Heart session, for example more self-confident and sovereign, in the presence of your loved ones you can't help but act like the little idiot everyone always considered you as.

If this is the case don't blame yourself. It is natural. Instead, use it: This gives you the opportunity to consciously feel the old emotions again and see what else they need from you or from whom you have taken them over.

Next time, just before the meeting remember the old feeling that trapped you and consciously watch it arise in the situation. Now you know that it is a feeling and not a fact,

Nothing is dangerous about feeling it. Carry it in your heart (and not only in your head); in your heart it is safe like a little child in your arms! Face the situation by feeling it, taking care of it, letting it be present in your heart. You will see that this is exactly what will bring about a change.

Finding the right decision

You have to decide between A and B - or between several possibilities. You don't know which is the right thing to do. First consider: What does "the right thing" mean for you, in what sense should this decision be right? Clarify that first. Because no decision is right or wrong in an absolute way. It can be right or wrong only in relation to a particular goal. You have a job offer in New York and one in Truro: What is important for you? Earning a lot of money, having a fulfilling job, a friendly, human environment, a pleasant atmosphere, cultural events, good restaurants, being close to nature... and other things. Once you've clarified that, the first and maybe decisive step towards finding the right decision is done.

If you find yourself unable to decide, use the Keys to the Heart method in the following way:

First take care of the emotional state that is at the forefront of your mind. How does it feel in your body to be unable to decide, to not know which way to go? Which emotion comes up?

Indecisiveness, feeling torn…?

Get to know this feeling and check what it needs from your heart.

Next step (if possible, wait at least 24 hours before you start the second step):

Let's call the different options you have "A" and "B".

Now imagine that you have chosen option A,

and apply the method to it (body awareness - emotion - heart).

Do the same with B (and any other options).

Emotions often stand in the way, so that you can no longer recognise what is emotion, what is the voice of the heart and what is intuition. Applying the Keys to the Heart steps helps you out of this confusion and to find the right decision.

Healing old emotional wounds

"Emotional wounds" is the common expression for that which hurts us deep inside and which goes normally back to events from our childhood that shocked and hurt us.

That which is hurt is not ourselves, but the image we have of ourselves. This image is formed in childhood. From the behaviour of our parents or other important caregivers, we read off who we are and what we are like. Remember: Daddy is angry, so I must be bad. Mummy has no time for me, so I'm worth nothing to her.

I must be worthless. All this is of course not true, but unconsciously we think it is. And this hurts us, because we are still convinced that we are bad, worthless and much more.

We are not aware of these convictions and therefore cannot question them.

An emotional wound also can occur when we do not get something that we expect to get according to our evolutionary expectations. For example, being carried against our mother's body until we can walk by ourselves, or being breastfed.

We bring expectations from the earth when we come into this world, and also expectations from heaven, the higher spheres where everything is innocence, love and beauty. If reality does not meet these expectations, it feels like a violation.

Our self-image, what we believe we are, is built up from all these experiences.

"I am someone who has no confidence, who is full of fair(?)."

Not having been carried on the body? Not feeling secure?

"I am not important, not loved, not wanted. I am never satisfied."

Not fed at the mother's breast?

And so on. Each one of us has a cocktail of basic beliefs most of which are negative. You are lucky if there are some positive ones among them!

If we were identified with our soul, which by definition is limitless, infinite, immortal and holy, nothing could hurt us. But since we are identified with our poor self-image and since this self-image is built upon our basic beliefs, behaviours, words, reactions of others can hurt us!

The Keys to the Heart process clears this up. Every aspect of your self-image, every emotional wound and every belief that goes with this pain will inevitably be illuminated sooner or later if you are consistent enough in applying the method to your daily life problems.

The emotional wound heals as soon as the pain is consciously and wholeheartedly felt. This acts as a healing balm. Of course, this is only true if you realise that it is a feeling and not a fact. No matter what circumstances may have triggered it and what facts have been its origin, in the Keys to the Heart process your attention is not on the circumstances, but on your body and your feeling.

Awakening from false beliefs

Every emotional wound is going together with a negative basic belief. The pain of the "wound" is the emotion, the belief the thought behind it. If I feel hurt because someone treats me like crap, I might suffer from the basic pain of humiliation or worthlessness, which is both, a thought and a feeling. If throughout my life I always have been convinced of having no right to exist I unconsciously believe that this is a fact, and this belief is in the same time a feeling, an emotion. And of course, I always and everywhere feel like someone who has no right. People feel that and treat me according to my conviction. This is what happened to myself. But one day, a small, ridiculously insignificant incident made me mad of anger. I was so upset that I instantly sat down and asked myself: What hurts me so badly that I get so angry? So, I discovered the pain of being unwanted and the related conviction of not having the right to exist. From this day on I became aware of this conviction in almost every situation I met, and discovered that I was used to behave as if I were unwanted and not entitled! And gradually this conviction lost its power and I began to behave in a different manner, more naturally, more confidently, surer of myself.

Getting rid of reaction and behaviour patterns

When you awake from a false belief, you start to change. It's a natural consequence. But you must know that our reaction patterns are like roads engraved in the matter of our brain, so that we happen to react in some situations in the old way although we awoke from the underlying thoughts and feelings. This is because the situation takes us by surprise and we don't have the time - or don't take the time - to "switch the light of consciousness on" and become aware of our emotions. This awareness would help us to willingly decide what we want to do instead of reacting automatically. But when we forget to switch this light on – well, then we have to look at the situation afterwards. Instead of watching, feeling, opening our heart in the middle of the situation, we fall into our automatic reaction – and have to look at it afterwards.

Example: My husband reacts coldly to a friendly and tender affection, and immediately I leave the room. Outside, I come to my senses and ask myself what caused me to act in this way. One minute of Keys to the Heart work, and I discover under some negative emotions (like anger, defiance, grief and revenge), the pain of being rejected.

Fleeing has always been my automatic reaction to rejection. But now, after this little "heart work", being rejected is no longer to me a fact but I know that it is just an idea I am identified with, together with the corresponding way of feeling. I "am" not rejected, I just feel this way. Maybe this opens my eyes and my heart to what's going on in my husband. Maybe he is worried about something or suffers from a headache.

So: if you want to get rid of a behavioural pattern, take a situation in which you have displayed this pattern and get to the bottom of it using the Keys to the Heart process: How does this feel in your body, how do you feel, what does this feeling need from your heart. Apply the 10 keys.

For a while the old pattern might still reel off, but you'll become aware of it while experiencing the situation, and little by little it will give way to new possibilities of behaviour.

Clarify and harmonise relationships

Applying the Keys to the Heart method to whatever problem you have in your relationships will of course clarify and harmonise them, even if you are the only one who applies the method.

Little by little you will realise what you project on the other person. You begin to take an interest in the reality of the other person instead of perceiving her or him only in relation to what you expect from this person. You will even be able to open your heart and feel how she feels instead of rejecting these feelings or taking them over as you probably did before.

In the meantime, while you are still projecting but start to become aware of it, you can even use this projection: For instance, if your (new) partner triggers in you the same reactions that you had in your childhood to your father, discovering this will give you an opportunity to clarify your relationship with your father. Just apply Keys to the Heart to every incident that elicits these childish reactions! And by doing so, don't forget to check in the end if some of the feelings you discover do not belong to your father, to eventually give them back.

This will not only free you and your partner from your projections onto him, but also free you from your projections onto your father - who is or was not only your father, but also his own person. Discovering this will open your heart for him.

Now you may ask whether it doesn't take two to sort out a two-way relationship?

Of course, it is more than nice, it's even marvellous when both partners apply Keys to the Heart to relationship problems. But it also works if you are the only one who practices. Not everybody has the desire, the disposition, the patience or the motivation for this. (Unfortunately, motivation for inner work usually arises through suffering). If you yourself wake up from your false convictions and therefore don't have to react emotionally to everything, you are less dependent on the behaviour of the other person, and that is a great liberation for you as well as for your partner.

And what is more, your heart opens up, you can feel the partner's feeling and your heart reacts to them with understanding, respect and compassion. Thus, you will experience a relationship which is warmer, more beautiful, more fulfilling, even if the person you're with doesn't change that much.

And if you notice that you desperately want him or her to change, remember that this is another opportunity to get into the Keys to the Heart process in order to find out why it is so important to you, what it does to you if he or she does not change, what exactly you are longing for and how you feel when you imagine that your partner indeed changes... And recognize all these feelings as what they are – feelings – and open your heart to them. You will discover that you do not depend as much as you believed on the other's behaviour. Small we are dependent on the behaviour of our parents, because we cannot yet exist on our own. But as adults we are not really dependent on the behaviour of our partners (except when we need them for our physical care, for example because we are seriously ill).

If we think we are, it is due to childish projection, so some inner work is needed!

All this applies, mutatis mutandis, not only to our intimate relationships, but also, to those with our friends, colleagues, superiors, employees, and other acquaintances. The Keys to the Heart work clarifies misunderstandings, prejudices and projections and clears the way for real relationship (heart to heart instead of projection to projection).

Overcoming fears

Some fears can be easily overcome through the Keys to the Heart method because they refer to something past, and not to the actual situation (as a child, you have experienced abandon, rejection, injustice or humiliation, and the pain together with the fear of it is still in your body and is triggered by the actual situation). Of course, you don't know that in the beginning of the process, but you'll find it out in the end when you discover the pain under the fear (that which you are afraid of). Once you open your heart to this pain you realise that it is a feeling (and a thought) and not a fact. These fears mostly need keys like "understanding", "permission", "compassion" and "to be perceived as a feeling and not a fact".

But some fears really relate to the actual situation and aim to protect you from a real danger. This kind of fear often needs the key "being perceived", and "be noticed". Often, they also need "appreciation". These fears have an important function. They do not need to be overcome, they want to be perceived and noticed!

Feeling the fear consciously (and knowing that it is a feeling and not a fact) will make you attentive, vigilant, mindful. Whereas, staying identified with this fear will hypnotise you and make you blind for possibilities and opportunities.

Learning to feel again

Many people come to my workshops with the intention to "learn to feel again". This issue is so important in our culture that I even wrote a book called "Learning to feel again" ("Wieder fühlen lernen"), not yet translated. It's mostly men who come with this request. And this is exactly what Keys to the Heart is about. In my native language, German, the name of this method is "Körperzentrierte Herzensarbeit", "body-centered heart work". Feeling begins in the body, because this is where feelings are expressed – and this is where we can re-discover them when we have suppressed and forgotten them. This is why I called my heart work "body-centered". You can't feel abstractly, mentally, you have to feed physically. That is what connects body and mind.

Applying the Keys to the Heart process to all the issues you are dealing with will help you to learn to feel (again).

Paying attention to your feeling will make you aware not only of your emotions and those of others, but also of instinct and intuition.

And even more:

Feeling is what makes you alive.

That is why so many people long to "learn to feel again".

Alleviate and heal physical symptoms

Most physical complaints have an emotional core. (If not, they are at least accompanied by emotions. Being sick or suffering from physical pain does something to you.) All medical traditions know this, and I myself have experienced and observed countless times how in symptoms like back pain, heart problems, stomach ache, even toothache repressed feelings can be traced, and how the symptoms improve or sometimes disappear completely, after applying the Keys to the Heart method.

The procedure is the same as that explained in the practical part, only you leave out the first step (topic and initial situation), instead you start the exercise right away with the bodily state.

This is the way you proceed:

Experience your body symptom with full attention while feeling your breath,

Then turn your attention towards the emotion by watching what feeling or feelings

are hidden in this symptom or emerge while experiencing the bodily state. Get to know these feelings, one after the other, thoroughly, feel them, and check the key words in order to open your heart. See if perhaps you need to give the feeling(s) back to someone because you once unconsciously took it over from that person.

Then return back into body awareness:

What has changed?

Continue until the symptom has clearly changed or you feel that it is enough (for today?).

Useful hints: Sometimes many different feelings express themselves in one symptom or one part of the body. In this case you have to patiently explore this symptom by feeling it again and again until you discover the bottom of the problem. At some point you will have discovered the core emotion and then you'll realise that the body lets them go.

Sometimes it's hard to discover the feelings that are hidden in a symptom when you don't have a topic for it. You don't see which circumstances they are related to, and thus might find it difficult to discover the right name of the emotion. Let's take back pain for example. If as topic and initial situation I take the fact that I'm always overworking myself with computer work, then it's easy for me to discover in the back pain a feeling of "strain" or "overload". If, however, I simply take "back pain" as the initial topic, without knowing which kind of situation, it has to do with, it can be more difficult to recognise the feeling hidden in it.

Keys to the Heart process with a topic as starting point: Emotions (=feelings) easy to recognise.

Topic and initial situation: "Spend too much time working at the computer".

Body symptom: back hurts

Feeling in it: tortured, overstrained

Heart key: wants to be seen, noticed, felt and taken care of (mercy)

Body symptom: less hurting

Keys to the Heart process starting directly with body symptom, without topic/situation as a start: Recognising feelings might be more difficult

Topic and initial situation: back pain

Feeling in it: ?? "I don't know, it just hurts"

Heart key: ??

This is how I proceed in cases like this:

Topic and initial situation: Back pain

Feeling in it: ??

Think of life situations: While you continue to feel your back pain, fade in life circumstances: work, home, relationship, family, finances ... whatever is actually part of your life. Watch which thought makes your back more noticeable.

Continue thinking about this topic or situation while continuing to feel your back pain. Now it should be easier for you to recognize and name the feeling it expresses.

If there is no way for you to discover and name the feelings which are hidden in your bodily symptom, just stay with the symptom, be present right in there, feel your breath and take care of it by simply being present. Very often this is exactly what it needs.

Finding more self-love and inner security

Every single step in the Keys to the Heart process is taking care of yourself. Each time you open your heart for a feeling that you had forgotten, repressed, overlooked, banished from your heart, it is as if a part of you comes back home.

Little by little, this creates a kind of inner security even if you continue to experience challenging situations or heavy emotions. You become less dependent of what others do or think, you enjoy your own presence and you find your guideline in yourself, in your own heart.

Little by little you will develop tolerance, understanding and even respect for yourself, judge yourself less harshly, and perhaps even discover a kind of love for the person you are.

And little by little you will develop tolerance, compassion and even respect for others, judge them less harshly, and develop understanding for them. In other words, you will be able to open your heart to other people.

Understanding the feelings of others

After having opened your heart to an emotion, you can encounter the same kind of emotion in others without having to flee, to fight against it or to close your heart to that person. So, the more feelings you discover within yourself and bring into your heart, the more understanding you automatically develop for others. You know their feelings because you have experienced them, so your heart stays open and reacts with compassion, understanding and respect. Moreover, you will often feel them directly.

And every time you give an emotion back to the person from whom you took it over, your heart opens up to that person and you finally understand how they feel or have felt! It's in that very moment of the "return to sender" that your heart reacts with understanding, compassion or respect.

Sometimes I even add these keywords that appear in my heart to the emotion that I return to its owner.

Opening your heart

Thus, with each Keys to the Heart session your heart becomes a little bit more open for yourself and in the same time for others.

But let me clarify something. This new state of open-heart does not always correspond to what you might have imagined it to be! Someone can be sweet, reserved and shy in his behaviour and yet be closed in his heart, while another may appear to be rude, reserved and unfriendly and yet have an open heart!

To have an "open heart" simply means to be able to feel, instead of closing oneself off from feelings, neither your own feelings nor those of the people you meet. Opening your heart can make you friendlier and more tolerant. But it can also mean that you have the courage to be more honest and more truthful! If I have an open heart for a friend, who behaves foolishly and inconsiderately, I'm in a position to read him the riot act. If my heart is not open, I am not able to do this because I am identified with my fear of upsetting him or losing him!

When the heart is open, it feels, and when it feels, it is alive.

Ending conflicts or making them superfluous

This is a great area of application for the Keys to the Heart method. Whether you are in the middle of a conflict or feel that a conflict starts to arise: Say "stop" to yourself. "Stop" means: Wake up. Take a deep breath and turn your attention towards yourself. Feel your body. Become aware of your actual feeling, try at least one or two "heart keys". Check whether it belongs to your counterpart, by giving it back. This does not take extra-time; it can be done in the middle of a discussion and nobody has to realise it.

In heavy conflicts there is always a taking over of feelings, often like a ping-pong: A does something, B gets angry, A takes over B's anger and so forth, and each time the anger gets bigger – until it comes to an explosion or an awakening. You can be the one who awakes, simply by turning your attention away from your counterpart and feeling your own feelings as described before. Normally you'll find that the deeper feeling that is triggered in you is a pain from the past, and very often the other person suffers from the same pain. The reason for the escalation is normally not a fact but an old feeling. Therefore, once you have discovered and maybe given back this feeling, the tension releases and you can relax. If necessary, you will now be able to present your point of view in a calm and clear way, with respect for yourself and for the other person's feelings. You might even be more open to what the other party has to say and be able to find a solution.

But if it's war and you can't retire from it for important reasons, the Keys to the Heart process will help you stay centred, clear and awake.

When you apply the method on a conflict, don't forget to look out for what you long for or which is your own desire. What is it you want to reach, to get, to achieve, what is your goal? Make this clear for yourself, and then feel and sense this longing and check what it needs from your heart.

Keys to the Heart can also help to solve inner conflicts. There are two parts of you that cannot be reconciled with each other. Let's call them A and B.

A wants this, B wants that. Each part has his own feelings. The exercise is to get to know 'A's feelings and then 'B's feelings and to open your heart to each of them.

But first of all, look at the emotion that actually dominates you, the 'AB'-feeling so to say: How it feels to be in this conflict. Maybe torn, or indecisive or confused.

Open your heart to this feeling. Often it needs "space" as key – which also means time. If this is the case, actually give it space and time before you continue.

Now, take care of A: First of all, identify with A and let A express his/her desire. Apply the Keys to the Heart steps with each of the feelings A presents. Then repeat the same procedure with B. It is as if you had two children arguing with each other, and you say: Stop! I will listen to both of you, one after another. Who is first?

First A, then B. What does A say, what does A want? Express aloud or in your mind

A's thoughts, then tune into your body and, one by one, discover your unconscious feelings

in your body sensations. Check for each one of the Heart Keys.

When A's feelings are in your heart, do the same thing with B. Maybe another day. Same procedure. Let B have his say. Body, emotion, heart. Until all the important feelings have what they need.

In the end you will see: Even if your mind cannot reconcile A and B, your heart can.

Developing Emotional Stability

The emotional stability you can develop through Key to the Heart work is not a static state of equanimity and serenity in which nothing can upset you. It rather consists in the discovery of a secure platform within yourself to which you can escape when an emotional storm hits. From this platform you can allow and experience all your feelings fully without being drowned in them.

This platform is called conscious awareness.

Finding a higher perspective

In order to apply the Keys to the Heart process you have to be in a higher than the normal perspective. But this higher perspective is nothing mystical, you reach it by simply switching to "being aware" instead of "being identified". When despair overwhelms you: instead of thinking "I am desperate", say to yourself "Aha, there is despair." This altered formulation lifts you into a higher perspective. Now you are able to take care of that feeling instead of drowning in it.

At the end of a successful Keys to the Heart session, when you went completely through your problem and got to its bottom, you will often experience moments of enlightenment, of deep peace, or of full realisation. Now you are really in a higher level of consciousness, even if this is not at all what you were searching.

Be careful, however, not to fall into the trap of identification here. This wonderful new feeling is also a feeling, take it for a feeling and not for a fact, and open your heart to it! Feel it, explore it consciously and check what it needs from your heart. Very often this beautiful or high feelings need to be felt not just a moment, but again and again so that they find their place in your heart. If you take it for a fact and identify with it – now I am enlightened -, the wonderful experience will disappear like every experience. But if you recognize it as a feeling and take it into your heart, it really belongs to you, because all it takes to experience it again is to remember how it feels! This new feeling needs attention like a young plant needs water.

Take this new feeling consciously into your daily life, remember this feeling in certain situations, and observe how it affects you! If you practice this consistently, it will change your charisma, your self-image, your relationships, your life in a positive way.

Coming to serenity

Serenity is an attitude that comes about when you stop taking things too seriously or importantly.

It is not to be confused with the resigned bitterness of the elderly person who has seen all her hopes dashed in the course of her life and therefore thinks that nothing matters anyway!

Applying the Keys to the Heart method might lead to an attitude of serenity. But if this is so, don't forget that this attitude is also a feeling, and if it arises don't forget to feel it consciously and to open your heart to it! Just treat it like every other feeling. Serenity often arises of its own accord at the end of a successful Keys to the Heart session. If this is the case, don't just say: "Wow! Now I'm relaxed!" but get to know the body state and feeling of being relaxed and open your heart to it!

If you want to achieve and maintain serenity as a kind of fact, you are again unilaterally identified with one feeling - instead of simply noticing and getting to know every feeling that arises. You end your journey of awakening, when it hasn't really begun yet! There is still so much beauty to discover, not only serenity, but also enthusiasm, not only detachment, but also commitment, not only equanimity, but also love ... So many nuances of feelings waiting to be discovered and to be felt!

Initiate and support spiritual awakening

"Keys to the Heart" is an excellent support for spiritual practice. The heart is the door to heaven. Very often people suppress their emotions in the name of spiritual refinement which leads directly to hell because they close the door to heaven.

Moreover, the Keys to the Heart method, if practiced consistently, turns out to be a path in itself.

Getting rid of extraneous burdens you have put on yourself

It is unbelievable how quickly your emotional life and behaviour can change when you free yourself from those feelings you took over from your parents or other important persons.

Sometimes you discover one single feeling or a little group of feelings that you have taken over, let's say, from your mother, but sometimes it is a whole complex of feelings including pain and basic convictions that you will recognised as not belonging to you and return to sender.

When you come to the step "Returning foreign feelings" in the Keys to the Heart process, don't think about who the feeling in question could be taken over from, but rather imagine all the persons in question plus a figure representing "unknown", and observe what happens! If you give the feeling to the right person(s), you will clearly notice it.

The burden slides off you.

This is the beginning of a new life where you start to discover your own desires, your own feelings, your own way.

How the Keys to the Heart Process can help you fulfil your longings

As soon as you open your heart to a longing that you have previously ignored or suppressed, you will notice something interesting. In the very moment you apply the correct key to your heart, you suddenly have an inner certainty that you are now on your way to having this longing fulfilled, even if your mind has no idea how this is going to be possible.

You can enhance this aha-moment by venturing one step further. As I explained before: Imagine that your wish has been fulfilled and discover the positive feeling that results from it. Open your heart to this feeling by offering all the keys, with the most important one being "recognising it as a feeling a opposed to a fact". When this key clicks into place, the penny will drop for you, making you realise that this is what you *really* always wanted: this feeling. You always thought that first you needed this particular outer situation, this thing or this person, in order to generate this feeling; yet now you have discovered this feeling already within you. You realise that feeling this feeling was always at the heart of the matter – it was just that you were completely clueless about it. You neither knew that it was all about this feeling, nor that this feeling was already within you. Now that you have discovered it, you simply need to hold this feeling in your heart and remember to feel it often.

If you tend to this feeling by remembering it regularly, if you cultivate it within you, it gradually becomes a natural way of feeling, it suffuses you, it alters your way of being, your posture, the energy-flow throughout your body, your thinking, your behaviour, your aura. In this way your frequency will

go into resonance with the matching outer reality –
you have become compatible with your wish.

Example: Emma the poor

*Emma has grown up in poverty. She has learned that the poor
live in their own world and that the world of the rich is
unattainable. She is identified with poverty: "I am poor". As
"Emma, the pauper" she looks upon the world of the rich
with both longing and envy. When in the company of affluent
people, she feels uncomfortable, not at home, not accepted -
and this is exactly how she is perceived by them. It's palpable
that she does not belong - poverty seems stamped onto her
forehead.*

*In her Keys to the Heart session Emma opens her heart to
the feelings of envy, longing and hopelessness and then
discovers that she has taken these feelings on from her parents.
She hands them back to them and in her imagination also
suggests that her parents may want to pass them back to their
ancestors. She repeats the same process for the underlying
feeling of worthlessness. Her longing for riches requires mainly
the key "being freed of the idea of impossibility". Next, she
vividly imagines being rich and discovers that at the base of it
all she wants to feel valuable.*

*For a few weeks Emma practices feeling valuable, to
consciously feel precious wherever she goes. One day she is
invited by a former schoolmate to an event in a very affluent*

area. She is accepted without any problems and she herself feels as if she belongs. Emma starts talking about a business idea that she developed during her many longing day-dreams, and because she now has the right contacts, the right charisma, and the support of her school friend, she can implement her plans with ease. Money starts flowing in soon after and she can now afford to replace the expensive dress that she had borrowed from her friend with one she has bought herself.

Opening your heart to your longing and the positive feeling connected to its fulfilment, plus giving it plenty of attention, basically means that you are no longer desperate for its fulfilment, as you already have the most important thing: the positive feeling. This gives you a personal and practical experience of what the wisdom teachers of all traditions have been saying all along: what you seek already exists, and it exists within you. It's just that now it's not some general philosophical insight for you, but a concrete, personal experience that changes your life for real. As a consequence, it will hopefully also entice and encourage you to continue on this path of feeling your feelings, your body and your heart.

Books by Safi Nidiaye on the Keys to the Heart method

in German: Der Schlüssel liegt im Herzen,
Driediger Verlag 2020.
(The German translation of the present English book.)

Gefühle sind zum Fühlen da,
Integral/Penguin Randomhouse,
2017.

Die 10 Herzensschlüssel,
Gräfe und Unzer 2014.

Das befreite Herz,
Ullstein Allegria 2012.

Der entscheidende Schritt,
Ullstein Allegria 2010

Aufwachen und lachen,
Integral 2005.

Herz öffnen statt Kopf zerbrechen,
Integral 2004.

Das Tao des Herzens,
Ariston/Hugendubel 2002.

in Spanish: Abrir el Corazon en vez de romperse la cabeza.
Ediciones Obelisco 2013.

in Italian: Usa il cuore non la testa,
Punto d'Incontra 2011.

in Polish: Otworz Serc Zamiast Lamac, Sobie-Glowe, Wydawnictwo,
Hartigrama 2014

Klucz znajdziesz w Sercu.
Rozwiązywanie problemów poprzez świadome odczuwanie.
Wydawnictwo Centrum 2022

Videos in English on YouTube:

https://www.safi-nidiaye.com/safi-english/

About Safi Nidiaye

Safi Nidiaye is one of the best-known German speaking authors on psychology and spirituality. Since 1990 she has written about 30 books, some of which have been translated into Spanish, Italian, Polish and Turkish. This is the first book making her work available in the English language.

Safi's most popular books include *"Love is more than an emotion"* (Liebe ist mehr als ein Gefühl, 1990), *"The voice of the heart"* (Die Stimme des Herzens, 1998), *"Open your heart instead of racking your brain"* (Herz öffnen statt Kopf zerbrechen, 2005) and *"Feelings are there to be felt"* ("Gefühle sind zum Fühlen da", 2017).

At the centre of her work is her signature Keys to the Heart process – a methodology based on Zen meditation. She has developed this body and feeling awareness process since the early 1990s and taught it in workshops and seminars both for personal use and to enhance the work of countless psychotherapists, medical doctors, healing practitioners, social workers and school teachers.

For more information on books, workshops, videos and contact for English speaking activities visit: **www.safi-nidiaye.com**

www.ingramcontent.com/pod-product-compliance
Lightning Source LLC
Chambersburg PA
CBHW051349280526
45784CB00007B/2875